BOAT COSMETICS MADE SIMPLE

BOAT COSMETICS MADE SIMPLE

How To Improve And Maintain

A Boat's Appearance

By
Sherri Board

Second edition, completely revised

TUG PRESS

P.O. Box 15188, Newport Beach, CA 92659

Edited by James A. Ayers,
consulting editor for the national headquarters of the National Writers Club, owner/managing editor
of Criscadian Editorial Services, Aurora, Colorado

Illustrated by Barnes Art Service, Santa Ana, California

Published by Tug Press

10 9 8 7 6 5 4

Boat Cosmetics Made Simple. Copyright © 1989 by Sherri Board.
Copyright © 1991 by Sherri Board. Second edition copyright © 1993,
completely revised, by Sherri Board. Copyright © 1996 by Sherri Board.

The information and advice contained in *Boat Cosmetics Made Simple*
are the opinions of the author which she shares in good faith. The
author and publisher of, and professional contributors to this book,
however, cannot accept responsibility for any damage which may result
from following the advice given herein.

ISBN 0-9634767-8-5 (previously ISBN 0-930030-56-7)

DEDICATION

This book is dedicated to my best friend,
Sue Jones, for her patience in dealing
with my abnormal obsession to clean boats;
for her unselfish willingness to push a brush
whenever I was in a pinch;
and, for listening to me
throughout the writing of this book.

Also, to my family.
Each member inspires me more than they know.

ACKNOWLEDGEMENTS

I want to thank the following people who took time out of their busy schedules to offer their kind and expert advice. Furthermore, I would like to include a very special thanks to my mentor and friend, Bill Beck. He took me under his wing when I was an amateur boat maintenance worker, which truly helped to develop me into the professional I am today.

Timothy Allen Board, B.S.
Critic and my safe haven

Kathy Barnes-Million
Illustrator and a great inspiration

Bill Beck
Professional boat maintenance worker

Chuck Reed
Compounding and waxing

KC Underwater Yacht Service
Bottom Cleaning

Odessey Marine and Diving Services
Bottom Cleaning

Aqua Marine Sail Cleaning
Maintenance of sails and covers

Lillian T. Hanniff
Secretary of the Los Angeles Maritime Museum

Michael A. Cropper
Librarian/ Archivist of the Los Angeles Maritime Museum

D.K.'s Donuts of Tustin, CA
The best company, coffee, and doughnuts around!

TABLE OF CONTENTS

INTRODUCTION

With the second edition of *Boat Cosmetics Made Simple* comes many exciting changes. There is much more step-by-step information on how to take care of your teak, how to make minor gelcoat repairs, and some more advice from our friendly "dock rats." These are just samples of the many changes made in this edition.

Another change you will notice is a difference in attitude toward our environment. The biggest change has been our awareness of the damage that is being done to our marine environment. Close to my home, the waters around Santa Monica Bay and Marina del Rey are unswimmable. To me, not being able to swim in a natural environment like the ocean is disgusting and we must do our part not to dump cleaning products that are not biodegradable into our waters. It is against the law to do so! If you are not sure how to dispose of chemical waste properly, please call the agency that picks up your garbage every week or the Environmental Protection Agency. These agencies should be able to direct you.

This second edition, however, greatly emphasizes using biodegradable products. If you are hooked on a product that is not biodegradable, drop the manufacturer a note asking him to look into making it so. Keeping your boat on a regular maintenance program will eliminate the need for harsh products. Indeed, products used for preventive maintenance are a lot easier for our environment to digest than those harsher products needed for restoration.

In conclusion, I want to reiterate that in writing this book, I do not pretend to know all the answers, nor do I claim that my way is the only way. There is no "only way." I share these methods with you because they have worked best for me and I hope they do the same for you. I delight in hearing other ways of doing boat maintenance and if you have ideas you would like to share, or you want to contribute to "Dock Rat Bits," send your comments to the publisher.

Remember: The hard part is not the preventive maintenance; it is the restoration after neglect.

Sherri Board (alias "Sher")
Newport Beach, California 1993

Welcome aboard mates.
Stand by for your instructions.

CHAPTER 1

TO KNOW HER IS TO MAINTAIN HER

Sher's definition of boat maintenance:
"Attending to all her cosmetic needs because
she deserves to float in beauty, not drown in ugliness."

Before we dive into the how to's of boat cosmetics, I thought it might be helpful to take a quick dip into some nautical history. Indeed, my motive for doing so is to help you realize (if you do not already) how fortunate we are today to have the luxuries and safety features our boating forefathers did without. I believe that if we compare the boat's past to her present, we might better appreciate the great changes that have been made for our comfort and safety.

She has become a lady of deep refinement — on your behalf, I might add. Treat her as such.

FLOATING BACKWARDS

For just a moment, pry yourself from your twentieth century boating luxuries (whatever they might be - fiberglass, electronics, antifouling paint. . .) and, let your mind float backward in time. Imagine it is 1492 and you are Captain Christopher Columbus. You have just been given charge of three ships: the Santa Maria, the Pinta, and the Nina.

Even though you do not own these ships (they were purchased by Queen Isabella of Spain), you realize the tremendous responsibility of this command: Without maintenance aboard, the ships and crew will not endure the demands of the sea.

So, being the incredibly ingenious captain that you are, you assign each ship the following men: painters, woodworkers, metalworkers, caulkers, and deckhands. This assures, not only the crew's safety, but that the ships will return to the queen in Bristol fashion.

Today, your attitude concerning boat maintenance should be just the same as the intelligent Captain Columbus'. Whether you choose to maintain her yourself or hire professionals, all aspects of boat maintenance should be performed on a regular basis.

Had Columbus' wife worn a watch, he might have coined the phrase his boating brothers conceived years later: "A ship is like a lady's watch, always out of repair."

HER RESUME FOR LOVE

The words that follow are pieces of your boat's past; a partial biography that hopes to show you some examples of her growth throughout time. Through the years, she has always been whatever seafarers have wanted her to be. This, in itself, should qualify her for much love and attention.

The Boat. Brace yourself. The boat does not have a baby book. No, as sad as it is, we can only speculate from crude drawings and a few phrases that the boat began its life millions of years ago as a log. And, as news of the log traveled to different parts of the globe, people used whatever was available to try out the new invention, such as, animal skins and/or clay.

Today, as you sit comfortably aboard your modern boat, envision exploring those magnetic waters the ways those ancestral boatsmen did: a caveman straddling a log; an Iraqi herdsman sitting on his knees in the center of an inflated goat skin; a New Zealand aborigine balancing on a bundle of reeds; or, as a Sindhi lying on his stomach over an opened-mouthed pot.

Which mode of transportation would you pick to cruise the Channel Islands?

Sailing. It is quite possible that sailing was discovered around 8000 B.C., when an Egyptian floating down the Nile river in a Fayoum boat, stood up, spread his arms, and let the wind fill his coat and push him along.

Do you suppose this man would have traded in his coat for some Dracon or Terylene sailcloth? You can bet *your* sailcloth he would have.

The Bilge. At first, rubbish talk amongst sailors was referred to as *bilge*. But one day long ago, some unknown sailor was sent to inspect the deepest, darkest, part of the ship where water and residue collect. After only a couple of minutes in this black hole, the sailor was truly convinced that this area was also rubbish. From that day on, the area where water collects in a boat has been referred to as *the bilge*.

The Bilge Pump. Have you ever wondered how our boating ancestors removed water from the bilge without an automatic bilge pump? It is a horrible thought, is it not?

An example of one way is through the use of a rotating, bucket-carrying, conveyor belt. The system took empty buckets down to the bilge and returned them to the top full of bilge water.

The Head. Long ago, this basic necessity was located forward on the ship's beakhead, which appropriately hung over a vast sea of water. Even though it was not the most private area to be in, the sea did a great job of reaching up and keeping it well washed down.

Anchor Cable Holes. Since her beginning, the boat has always been thought of as a woman. There was a time in history when she was consistently given eyes so she could see her way. The eyes were either painted on or carved into her bow.

As time sailed on, however, and the world modernized, the eyes of the boat turned into holes for anchor cables.

Starboard. Years ago, all Northern ship's steering, which consisted of one oar, was located on the right side of the ship, assuming one was looking forward. The steering side of the ship was first referred to as the *steerboard* side. Later, the word developed into *starboard*, meaning the right side of the boat.

Port. When a ship came into port to unload her cargo, she had to bring her left side up to the docks so she would not ruin her steering. The left side of the ship was first called the *load-board* side; then later became known as the *larboard* side. The problem with larboard was it sounded too much like starboard and confused the sailors when out at sea. Finally, someone suggested that the left side of a ship be called the *port side*. It stuck.

The Bow. Discovered by some Amazon tribe who realized if they streamlined the front of their *dugouts*, (hollowed out logs), they could cut through the water faster.

Gangway. The opening in the side of a boat at the head of an accommodation ladder that derived its name from the term *gangplank*. In

The Evolution of the Boat

1.

THE LOG

2.

LOG RAFT

3.

HIDE CORACLE

4.

LEATHER CORACLE

5.

DUGOUT

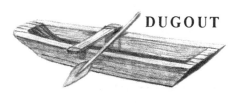

6.

RAFT OF POTS

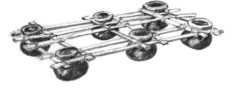

7.

INFLATED SKIN RAFT

8.
PAPYRUS BOAT

9.
EGYPTIAN SHIP

10.
STEAMBOAT

11.
SAILBOAT

12.
POWERBOAT

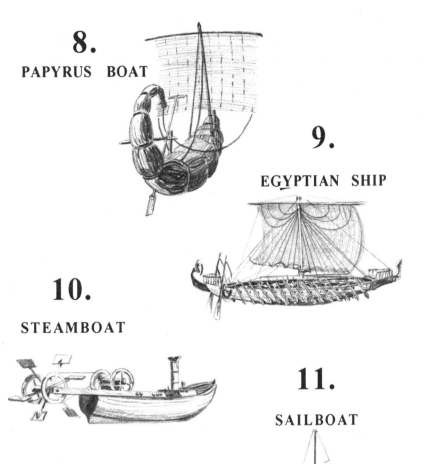

the days of pirate lore, it is believed persons who were no longer desired on board, such as those who did not do their maintenance chores, were told to, "Walk the plank!

MAINTAINING HER FUTURE

I can assure you: If you are maintaining your boat on a consistent basis, she will float proudly in recognition of the great technological strides that have been made and give you many years of enjoyment. But if she is sitting somewhere neglected, with her ego hurt, she is probably wishing she could go back to her simple life of being a log.

To be sure, this book will show you how to quell all her cosmetic demands and be a proud boat owner, not a mere bump on a log.

CHAPTER 2

WASH-DOWNS

Sher's definition of wash-downs:
"Hardworking bubbles powered by elbow grease
on a direct course to ensure her indefinite beauty. "

A boat should be washed down once a week, and/or, after each use. If harmful elements such as oxidation, air pollution, bird droppings, or salt and scum water are allowed to accumulate on the various surfaces, they eventually will become the proud new owners of the boat. And believe me, unlike the money you spent to purchase your boat, it costs these evil elements nothing to highjack it.

There is no excuse for a dirty boat. If you happen to be a busy boat owner, (perhaps you only have time for an occasional Sunday slip sail), hire a boat maintenance service, or a neighbor kid to wash down your boat for you. It is cheaper to pay for the service than to replace cloudy eisinglass or sick looking varnish. You will save money and you will feel better boarding a clean boat.

SUMMER VERSUS WINTER

Just because the boating season ends, does not mean the maintenance program should.

For example, although it is easier to continue maintaining a boat in the warmth of southern latitudes, do not neglect her just because you are in the middle of a cold, northern, season change. If your little toes are getting chilled, buy some warm socks and rubber boots and continue your regular maintenance program. If you are in an area where Mother Nature forces

On a direct course to ensure her indefinite beauty.

you to dry dock your boat, at least pay her a visit once a month to make sure she is OK.

WASH-DOWN GEAR

Limit the following items to wash-downs *only*. Ignore the desire to borrow something from your wash-down gear so that the next time you go to preform a wash-down, everything you need is readily available and not at home under a sink or flushed down a toilet somewhere. Store all your cleaning supplies in a bucket or dock box for easy access.

☐ Hose (as long as the boat)

☐ Bucket

☐ Hard and soft bristle brushes

☐ Mild, non-phosphate detergent

☐ 100% cotton rags

☐ Chamois ("The Absorber")

☐ Professional squeegee

☐ Elbow grease

BRUSHES

There are two types of bristle brushes I recommend for cleaning a boat. The first is a stiff polypropylene bristle brush which is good to use on non-skid, teak decks, and, perhaps, on a boat's waterline if it has a lot of build-up.

Keep in mind that this brush should be used only on surfaces that have been badly neglected. For example, a teak deck that has been pampered over the course of its lifetime need not be subjected to such harsh treatment. The polypropylene brush can be found in most marine hardware stores.

The second brush I recommend is the super-soft polyester bristle brush. Unlike the polypropylene brush, it is very gentle on paint, varnish, gelcoat, and glass windows. Oddly enough, I have never seen this type of brush in a marine hardware store. But, I have found them readily available in motor home supply outlets.

Regardless of the type of brush you are using, do your back a favor and buy a painter's handle or a telescoping extension pole. A painter's handle is quite a bit longer than the handles the brushes come attached to. My favorite is the telescoping extension pole. It is more expensive, but you can adjust this pole to whatever length you need. Any good hardware store will carry both types of poles.

RAGS

When I first started in the boat maintenance business, "rags" to me were my little brother's holey T-shirts and his outgrown Fruit of the Loom underwear. Back then, the thought of using these awkward articles on my boats sent me looking for another solution. Lucky for me and my shy self, I found one.

Actually, it was not me who found the answer at all. Rather, some other West Coast boat maintenance workers had looked to the babies of America for the answer and found it: Diapers.

Diapers make perfect sense, do they not? Think about it. What could be softer or, for that matter, more absorbent than what goes against a baby's precious behind? The diaper will do for the boat's various surfaces what it does for the baby's bottom: It will be gentle and at the same time absorb liquid.

If you have a diaper service in your area, you can purchase used diapers by the pound for a reasonable price. (Do not worry, they have been washed). Buying from a diaper company is much cheaper than purchasing the diapers from a marine hardware store.

If, however, you do not have a diaper service in your area (or perhaps you have never heard of one), use rags that are 100% cotton fiber. You will find that most fibers today are designed to repel water, not absorb it. So, pay close attention when choosing your rags. Cotton rags will make your job a lot easier and, most of all, be kinder to your boat.

LAUNDERING YOUR RAGS

I never gave much thought to washing and drying a bunch of boat rags until I heard about a fellow boat maintenance worker who did not either.

My associate was doing what he did every Sunday afternoon, laundering his rags in preparation for another week of wash-downs.

Everything was normal until the rags caught fire in the dryer. He realized immediately what he had done: He had mixed rags saturated with acetone with his regular wash-down rags. Acetone is flammable.

So, if you do not like surprises, keep wash-down rags separated from all the others. It is a good idea, and safer, to throw away any rags that might have harsh chemicals on them, but dispose of them properly. If you are not sure what "proper disposal" is, call your local dump. Your environment will appreciate your extra effort.

FOUNTAIN OF YOUTH

Washing down a boat with soft water is like spraying her with water from the Fountain of Youth. Using regular water, on the other hand, is like blasting her with water from the well of hard sediments.

Let us take a look down the well of hard sediments. Hard water contains excessive amounts of minerals, such as, iron, rock, clay, calcium and magnesium. How much depends upon where you live. Sometimes, the water can be so hard, it will etch glass. And, what about hard water spots? These miserable, crusty spots are just reminders that they dried faster than you did.

The answer to any ruination that hard water might cause (again, the severity being based on the area you live in) is to install a soft water system. A soft water system will filter out any harsh sediments and help you and your boat last longer. I have seen many soft water tanks sitting on docks throughout Southern California. A nice gentleman from Rayne Water said that they install many soft water tanks throughout the country. I am sure, whether your boat is stored in the water or at your home, your local water conditioning and softening agency would be happy to assist you. The cost is minimal. Make sure you put a nozzle on the end of your hose so all that wonderful water does not go to waste.

(**Important:** If you do use soft water, be sure you are also using a mild detergent. Most heavy detergents are made to react to hard water -- they may not know what to do in soft).

BOYCOTT PHOSPHATES

If your local government has not banned phosphates, you should. Phosphates can be found in many detergents, although it is not as prevalent as it once was because of our recent global environmental concern.

Whichever detergent you are used to using to clean your boat, check the box to see if it contains phosphates. If it does, throw it away -- now. There are many non-phosphate, biodegradable detergents on the market. I have had good cleaning success with the following: Joy, Lux, and Wisk.

Scientists do not know all there is to know of the affects that phosphates have on our marine environment. They do know that phosphates speed up the growth of a nuisance plant known to us as algae. Phosphates cause the algae to grow more rapidly and consume more oxygen, especially at night when there is no photosynthesis. Imagine being a school of fish whose only path to education is suddenly cut off by a bunch of green bullies.

HOSE DOWN SURROUNDING AREA

Before you start your wash-down, hose off any dirt on the dock or driveway. This will give you a clean environment to start with and eliminate tracking any dirt back onto your clean boat.

BATTEN DOWN THE HATCHES

There is nothing worse than finding an open window or hatch **after** you have washed down, especially if the boat does not belong to you. Before you turn the water on, check all windows and hatches.

Also, check the boat for obstacles that should not get wet. For example, it is easier to vacuum indoor-outdoor carpet than to wash it. Besides, a wet carpet is not something one wants to take on a Sunday bay cruise. Vacuum the carpet, roll it up, and put it in an area where it will stay dry.

CUSHIONS AND CONTROL PANELS

The following should be included in your wash-downs, except that you are not going to *hose them down*, you are going to *wipe them down*.

Vinyl Cushions. Wipe dirt and body oils off with a mild detergent and fresh water. Because these cushions absorb water like a sponge, do not flood them as if you were putting out a fire. Doing so will destroy the *cush*. And, nobody wants to be without *cush*, especially out in rough open waters.

Closed-Cell-Foam Cushions. If you are not sure the cushions on the boat are closed-cell-foam, sit on one. If it feels as though you are sitting on stacked BBs, it is closed-cell-foam.

These cushions are expensive, but they pay back in durability. Maintenance is the same for these cushions as it is for vinyl cushions with the exception that closed-cell-foam cushions cannot become water-logged unless there is a hole in them, which is why they make great life preservers.

Control Panels. Wipe control panels off with detergent and fresh water. Do not hose them off for the sake of convenience. Over time, doing so could cause internal damage.

WHERE IS THE WATER DRAINING, MATE?

Water exits a boat one of four ways: the scuppers, a bilge pump, a bailing bucket, or by pulling the plugs. So, make sure before you start the wash-down that you understand how the water will get out so it does not fill up around your ankles.

I knew of an unfortunate boat owner who, unknowingly, hired a "flash in the pan" to wash his 18-foot Shock Electric. Rather than filling a bucket up with water, Mr. Flash thought it would be easier to fill the boat up like a bathtub.

I am not quite sure how Flash got the water out of the boat (he probably thought it would evaporate), but I do know it was not by way of the bilge pump because when the boat owner went to turn on the motor the next day, the only sound that came out was, "Gurgle, gurgle, gurgle."

If the water has no way of getting out, do not put it in.

TOPKNOT DIRT

I served part of my apprenticeship as a boat maintenance worker washing down boats for a broker in Newport Beach, California. Her office was on the second floor which enabled her to view her boats and any person on them.

Well, one sunny April day, I was washing down a boat for the In-the-Water Boat Show. As I was proudly drying off the last water drop (I knew the boat would be the cleanest in the show) the broker yelled down from her balcony like a queen bee reprimanding one of her worker bees: "Sher, you didn't wash off the canopy!"

I climbed up the side of the boat and stood on my tip toes. Sure enough, there was a layer of dirt laughing back at me on top of the canopy. I had to rinse it off and watch it destroy my perfect wash-down.

Do not make the same mistake. Start from the highest point of the boat, check the top of it, and work your way down from there. Doing so will guarantee that dirty water will not cross a clean surface.

MILDEW

This green garbage grows like The Blob in warm, damp, dark places. It can usually be found on the shady side of a boat and normally appears during the humid summer months, invading a boat like tourists returning to their favorite sultry resort.

To combat mildew, use X-14 commercial mildew remover. You do not want this product to end up in the water or outside in your gutter. So, spray some X-14 on a dry cotton rag and wipe off the mildew. After the mildew disappears, wipe off the area with some soap and fresh water. **Do not get X-14 on painted surfaces. It is always wise to try X-14 on an inconspicuous part of the boat first to make sure it will not harm any surfaces.** I have never had any problem with this product.

Bleach also kills mildew. It is harder to work with, however, and can damage surfaces if it gets out of hand. If you are going to use it, dilute it with water and keep it confined to the mildewed area only. Do not let the bleach reach the beach! Dispose of properly.

To prevent mildew from returning, keep the boat clean, dry, and waxed.

TEAK TRIM AND DECKS

During your wash-down, scrub teak decks and trim. You will have to use your own judgement as to the type of bristle brush you want to use. For example, if the teak is not very dirty, use a soft bristle brush. If, on the other hand, the teak needs a good scrubbing, use a stiffer bristle brush. In either case, scrub across the grain of the wood, not with it. Scrubbing with the grain rips out the soft fibers of the wood. Your objective during a wash-down is to eliminate surface dirt, not the wood. (For monthly teak care, see Chapter 4, *Teak Tips*).

DEFENDING VARNISH: ENEMY OVERBOARD

If a varnished surface is not kept covered, it is always battling with two bitter enemies: dew and the sun.

Their strategy is simply one of moisture and heat. Hence, the dew, armed with acids and dirt, settles overnight on the sleeping varnish and waits for its accomplice, the sun, to rise. When the sun beats down on the dew, it magnifies the effectiveness of the dirt and acids, giving them extra strength to break down the varnish's resistance.

Your best defense against this process, besides keeping the varnish covered, is to wash the dew overboard. This will render the team defenseless, sort of like Popeye without his spinach.

SWABBING NON-SKID DECKS AND SWIMSTEPS

Sometimes, non-skid can be pretty tough to get clean, such as, after Uncle Fred spent the weekend dancing around the deck wearing his best black-soled church shoes and Monday morning you are faced with millions of black, scuff marks.

To remove stains of this type, try using a mild abrasive like Soft Scrub. (Soft Scrub comes in two types. Make sure you buy the kind without bleach or phosphates). Use it with a little bit of water and a stiff bristle brush. If the mild abrasive does not do the job, try some acetone. If you use tough abrasives, such as Ajax, over time such treatment will wear down your boat's non-skid decking.

If you find that the mild abrasive and acetone does not work, ask Uncle Fred to wear proper deck shoes!

DOCKLINES

Docklines are like the brakes on a car. They are needed for safety, but not thought of until they start to give out.

Some time during your wash-down, give the lines a gentle but thorough rinsing with a hose. It will eliminate dirt, salt and river scum which shorten the life of the lines.

TOPSIDES

The topsides should always be done last because no other part of the boat will be affected by the wash-down water running down their sides.

First, clean the waterline. Place your long-handled brush just above where the water hits the boat and scrub down into the water about a foot. This helps prevent growth from forming and makes for a fine looking waterline. (The person servicing your boat's bottom should be doing this, too. Read about this in Chapter 11, *A Tip Top Bottom*).

Scrub the rest of the topsides with a brush, fresh water, and a mild detergent. If it is a large boat, 32-feet or more, I recommend washing and rinsing off the detergent in sections so that it does not dry and leave a film.

If you cannot get to the other side of the boat to wash it, perhaps there is only docking on one side, the next time you go out, bring the boat into port differently so you can wash it. If you are a boat maintenance worker, communicate with the boat owner that the boat needs to be docked differently each week. This may seem logical to you, but I knew a boat owner who owned a 42-foot Spoiler. He loved his boat maintenance service until the day he brought his boat into port differently. For months, he docked with the starboard side to the dock. One day, however, he came into the port side. When he got off his boat, he noticed that the port side was covered with black soot and stains, (his boat was docked by an airport). It cost him a lot of money to get that port side back into shape because it never dawned on him that it was not being cared for.

If you are pulling your boat out of a river or lake, be sure to wash the bottom off with a brush, detergent, and plenty of fresh water.

Oxidation

If you notice a white film developing on the gelcoat, it is time for a compound and wax. (See Chapter 6, *Compounding, Waxing, and Repairing Gelcoat*).

If, however, you need to get rid of the ugly film for the moment, add three tablespoons of vinegar to your wash-down water to eliminate some of the oxidation. But, the vinegar is not a cure-all. Do not put off the inevitable.

Drying the Boat

The best tools to use for drying any boat are a professional squeegee and a chamois. (The "Absorber" works great).

Use the squeegee to pull the water off the various surfaces and follow with the chamois. For large, hard to reach surfaces, such as the topsides, attach the squeegee to an extension pole and pull away the excess water.

If it is a hot day and you are using hard water, wash and dry the boat in sections. Otherwise, the water will dry on the boat leaving hard water spots that are virtually impossible to get off. (Hopefully, you are on a boat that could be considered "a section" and you will not have this problem).

Waterways. Normally, after a wash-down, a boat will have some water build-up in its waterways, if it has any. Find the water and dry it. If a lot of water is left over, simply pull it through the scuppers with your squeegee. If you do not remove this water from the boat, it will stain fiberglass and cause wood rot.

Run the Bilge Pump

If you have access to the bilge pump switch, it is a good idea to run it after a wash-down. Leaving water in the bilge could cause a lot of unwanted damage.

Check the Interior

Always go below, if there is one, and check for leakage. Dry if wet. Notify the responsible party before the leaking can cause permanent damage. I have seen interiors destroyed because checking the interior after wash-downs went neglected. Do not pretend water is not there. Open windows if ventilation is needed.

Wings of Evil

During a wash-down on a 32-foot Grand Banks, I noticed tiny wings on the deck that looked like queen ant wings. I thought, perhaps, queen ants were allowed the luxury of boating.

In my inquiries, I learned that the tiny wings belonged to termites. I was astounded. I thought termites only had appetites for houses, not boats.

More often than not, when you notice these little creature's wings, they already have made a main course out of the boat's cellulose. They shed their wings when they have found good eating and they do not plan on flying anywhere else.

If you do notice these little wings on a boat, call a professional right

*Keeping your boat clean will help to prevent
the birds from making a nesting site of it.*

away. Do not wait until the termites become bigger than the boat.

Guano Got You Down?

For years, boat lovers have tried to come up with new ways of discouraging birds from dumping on their precious boats. For example, they have tried scaring them with owl figurines, snakes, and corn brooms. Some have even gone so far as making an example out of one by hanging it by its neck from the rigging. (Not a very humane thing to do, I might add).

Thus, being the perfectionist that I am, these scare-tactics were not keeping my boats clean enough. I decided to use bird psychology.

Unlike man's best friend, a bird dumps in its nesting site, and the more it dumps, the "sweeter" home is. So, I decided that maybe if I kept the bird bombs off my boats, the birds would go nest on the dirty ones. I was right.

I used a 22-foot Bayboat for my experiment because it was at the end of a dock with no boats to its port side and three very neglected boats to its starboard side.

I washed the Bayboat down weekly, each time removing bird droppings from the covers and dock area. I was amazed each time to find the boat clean while the others continued to get dirtier and "sweeter."

The birds sat on the other boats watching me, just waiting for the week that I would not show up.

Be Considerate

During the wash-down, if you happen to get water overspray on a neighboring boat, be considerate and dry it off. This is especially important if it lands on a boat that is well maintained.

I almost lost a good account because someone repeatedly left water overspray on my perfectly dried boat. It seemed as though I washed down my boat Friday morning and the boat next to mine got washed down Friday night. When the meticulous owner came down on Saturday morning, he was furious. At first, I thought I was going crazy. I always dry my boats. When I finally figured out what was happening, I dealt with the situation and did not loose my account.

I am sure this happens often. We all work hard to keep our boats beautiful. Maybe, if your boating neighbor sees you doing something amicable, it will catch on.

Are you sure you are using a clean rag?

CHAPTER *3*

DETAILS

Sher's definition of boat detailing:
"*Refining the little things on a boat*
to enhance the beauty of the whole floating investment."

Because all boats are thought of as women, maintaining her windows, cushions, stainless steel, etc., is like keeping makeup on her. Indeed, if these "cosmetic" needs are neglected, she will begin to look unkempt. (Remember: The older she is, the more attention she deserves).

A once-a-month application of the following suggestions will not only maintain the value of a boat, but will help her to stand out from all the rest, the envy of neighboring boat owners.

A Note of Caution

You will get better results from your detailing efforts if the boat is clean and dry before you start. Otherwise, the various surface types may become scratched. For instance, as you are happily polishing a surface, the dirt underneath your rag could be viciously destroying it.

Also, schedule your monthly detailing tasks to follow one of your weekly wash-downs. (See Chapter 2, *Wash-Downs)*.

Windows

I will be discussing the proper care for the following types of windows: glass, Plexiglass, and eisinglass. It may not seem important to treat these surfaces differently, but it is. They are quite different.

Keep in mind that even though the tender-loving-care methods vary, these surfaces all have the same worst enemy: **a dirty rag.** If there are any dirt particles in your rag, they will scratch and destroy all these surfaces quietly and unmercifully.

The sad part is that you do not notice the damage at first because the tiny, hairline abrasions are too fine to see. But after a million of them gang up on you, they will make you pay attention because you will not be able to see through the window.

Glass. Of all the glass cleaners on the market, plain old vinegar and water work the best -- a remedy nearly as old as the sea itself. Unlike some commercial glass cleaners, vinegar mixed with water will not streak or leave a film of any kind -- unless, of course, you add too much vinegar or the window did not come completely clean.

Pour one tablespoon of vinegar into a 32-ounce, plastic spray bottle and fill with fresh water. Squirt the solution onto one glass window at a time and wipe it off with a clean cotton rag.

Windows should be clear and sparkling. If they are not, there is something on them that should not be. For example, sometimes when heavy, salty fog mixes with dirt in the air it will stick to windows like a smoky ghost. You can see through the windows, but not clearly. This type of film is stubborn, but it will come off. It just takes a little more elbow grease.

Plexiglass. This acrylic material, more often than not, really takes a beating. I often wonder why boat builders put the stuff on a boat in the first place. I have done maintenance on an awful lot of boats and I would say only one boat out of ten had acrylic that was not damaged in one way or another.

Hence, I think the reason Plexiglass goes ignored is because boat owners and boat maintenance people think Plexiglass is hard and, therefore, tough enough. It is hard, but not tough enough, like everything else, to withstand a harsh marine environment. For instance, if Plexiglass is left dirty and unprotected, the sun will destroy it, turning it black and brittle. Another way Plexiglass is quickly destroyed is by using harsh chemicals on it, such as ammonia and acetone. For example, the window cleaner Windex is probably the most common window cleaner used in the home and on boats. But, Windex contains ammonia and when used on Plexiglass, the ammonia destroys it. Acetone eats Plexiglass. Ultimately, the Plexiglass becomes hazed and you will be unable to see through it.

Along with washing the Plexiglass during your wash-down, it should be polished once a month. There are a lot of good plastic polishes on the market. I prefer Sea Power's plastic polish and Novus plastic polish. Read the manufacturer's directions on the back. Using a clean dry rag, work the substance in a circular motion as opposed to back and forth. Light scratches can also be rubbed out with polishing.

I want to emphasize here: **Do not use window cleaner on Plexiglass. Most brands contain ammonia.**

Eisinglass. This term is used for the plastic-zippered windows found on a boat. Because they are made from vinyl, they scratch easily and deteriorate fast. As with Plexiglass, the scratches found in eisinglass are usually due to dirty rags -- such an unruly common occurrence.

Eisinglass is quick to show when it is being neglected. It will develop a milky white substance which is caused by the sun. In other words, it will begin to oxidize. If this sign is ignored, eventually you will be unable to see through the windows. (I am quite sure you have seen some pretty bad ones around because there are a lot out there).

A once-a-month application of a good plastic polish will keep the eisinglass looking great. If eisinglass is cloudy, use Novus plastic polish #2 to remove the oxidation. Follow-up with Sea Power's plastic polish.

A Bonus for the Fanatics

After glass, Plexiglass, and eisinglass surfaces have been cleaned, you can apply a clear polymer to them called Rain-X. Rain-X will adhere to all of these various surface types and will repel water and foreign matter from them like flies crash-landing on a sheet of ice. Visibility will be greatly increased, especially out at sea or skimming across a lake. Rain-X makes your maintenance chores easier and less frequent.

Rain-X can be found in most automotive stores. Follow manufacturer's directions on the back of the bottle. I cannot recommend this product enough.

Stainless Steel

Because of its unique characteristics, stainless steel is used extensively in the boat building industry. It is inexpensive, available, and virtually immune to rust and corrosion. Interestingly enough, stainless steel, when rubbed and polished, forms a hard surface skin. (This tough skin is due to the chromium content).

For the most part, boat builders use marine-grade stainless steel for their boats, most of which is on the high-grade scale. Most high-quality stainless steel can take a lot of neglect before it starts screaming for some attention, but do not let this attribute keep you from giving it any.

Once a month, clean the stainless steel with a good metal polish. I recommend Brite Boy, which has been around for years. I have compared it to a lot of other brands and I always go back to it.

After cleaning, apply a wax to the stainless steel. Not only will the wax add luster, but it will also blend in any scratches and repel water and foreign matter. Applying a wax to stainless steel also keeps hard water spots from forming. Remember, especially if the boat is used in saltwater, that the saltwater will take the wax off, so waxing needs to be repeated accordingly.

Rusted and Imperfect Stainless Steel

Stainless rusts because there is something foreign on it that it does not like. For example, when dew mixes with iron molecules in the air and settles on the stainless, it causes rust. The best prevention against rust is to simply keep the stainless wiped down -- especially keep salt off of it. If, on the other hand, you are faced with stainless steel which has already rusted, use some muriatic acid. **Be careful with this stuff.** If you spill the acid on the boat it will ruin it. Acid eats everything, boats, people, you name it. Get yourself a small throw away brush and dip it directly into the acid's container. Brush over the rust and wipe away with a bunch of paper towels. Dispose of the towels properly. Sometimes, stainless steel will develop little nodules, bumps, if you will. These are more than likely due to impurities in the stainless steel, or, just a low-grade stainless. (The causes of this phenomenon are being studied).

The most common areas for these nodules to appear are around the controls, fittings, antenna base, and the stainless steel rings around the gauges in a control panel. For these purposes, use the old stand by, Never Dull. If the nodules are not too bad, Never Dull will take them down some. But, if the problem has been ignored for a long time, Never Dull will only disguise them for a while. The imperfect parts should be replaced.

Chrome

Chrome is most commonly used on engine headers and boat trailer hubcaps. Chromed headers, left unprotected, will quickly turn a blue-red-black color, a result of the intense heat yielded by exhaust gases.

Thus, to keep headers clean and lustrous, they must be cleaned and polished after each use. **It is imperative that you let the headers cool first.** After the headers have cooled, use a damp rag and some mild detergent to wipe them down. Afterwards, polish them with a good chrome polish.

Chromed hubcaps can also take quite a beating, but can be kept up. It is important that when you rinse your boat off with fresh water after each use, you pay particular attention to the boat trailer, especially the hubcaps. Keep in mind that whether you are backing your boat into fresh or salt water, your trailer has been submerged into potentially damaging elements which must be thoroughly rinsed away. Keep the chromed hubcaps polished with a metal polish. It is good practice to keep a wax on them.

Brass and Bronze

There is nothing more elegant than polished brass and bronze and nothing more nautical than when they are left to tarnish. Like everything else, it is a personal preference.

Therefore, if a polished finish is desired, a lot of work must be sacrificed to keep it that way. Although, if you want the shine but not the work, a permanent clear coating can be applied to eliminate further oxidation. Also, waxing these metals slows down the oxidation process.

On the other hand, if the nautical oxidized finish is fancied, (that is the green or greenish-blue film that develops on these metals), no maintenance of any kind is required.

I know a boat owner who loves this patina with an added touch to it. He uses a 3-M Scotch-Brite pad, or "tuffy pad," on his brass hardware and scrubs off just enough oxidation to give the metal a brushed affect look, thus creating the illusion that something is being worn or used -- like Aladdin's lamp that only shined where he had rubbed it in the hope his genie would appear.

Oxidized Aluminum

(Note: Unlike all the other details in this chapter, this one does not have to be done once a month. Do only as needed).

Aluminum is the weakest of the metals so far discussed. Its surface skin is easily broken. When this happens, a chalky, white film forms on the aluminum's surface. Although this process does not hurt the metal, it is displeasing to the eye.

There are two things you can do to remedy this reaction. First, the aluminum can be sanded and a clear coating should be applied to cut off the air. Use whatever grit sandpaper is needed to remove the oxidation. Your second option, and one that is being done more and more, is to have the aluminum anodized.

Anodizing is an electrochemical process that forms a coating of aluminum oxide on the surface of the aluminum, sealing it off from oxygen and other harmful elements. Anodizing forms a hard, but porous layer so that the aluminum can be dyed if preferred. And, it is easy to maintain. Simply rinse it off with a mild detergent and water.

Cushions

Keep a good vinyl cleaner/restorer on the cushions. If you do not, the sun will dry them out and they will crack like peanut brittle.

Do not use an abrasive cleanser or harsh chemicals on the cushions. Doing so will destroy the finish before your eyes. Trust me, I learned the facts the hard way. Years ago, one of my first accounts was with a boat yard in Dana Point Harbor in California. I was given a 32-foot Sea Ray that looked like it had never seen detergent and water. It did not bother me, however, because I was set to make the boat look brand new, i.e., create a miracle.

To begin my miracle, I decided to start with the worst looking things on the boat, the cushions. They were so filthy, I ran up to the marine supply store for some reinforcements: Comet, bleach, spot remover, and a hard bristle brush. After scrubbing for half a day, the cushions finally gave in to my drastic measures.

At the end of the day, the owner of the boat yard came down to inspect the boat. He looked at the cushions in shock. He did not hesitate to inform me that the layers of dirt I had so diligently scrubbed off were in actuality the gray-blue finish of the vinyl. (I was fortunate he was so understanding because it would have taken me two days work to replace those sticky-clean cushions).

Moreover, if you want the cushions to last forever, keep them below deck or have covers made for them. Keeping them dry and out of the sun will preserve them indefinitely. If, however, the cushions have to be kept outside, stand them up on their zippers. This will allow any moisture trapped inside to drain down and escape out the zipper.

Plastic Instrument Panels

If there is a plastic instrument panel on the boat, I hope there is also a cover for it. Even an old towel or blanket would do. These types of panels take an awful beating from the sun and dry out quickly and crack. For its preservation, keep a good plastic cleaner/restorer on it.

Lifelines, Fenders, and Shore Power Cords

(CAUTION: Unplug the shore power cord before cleaning it. Acetone and lacquer thinner are flammable and could cause a fire if it is run across an exposed electrical wire).

Use acetone or lacquer thinner to clean all these items. Dampen a clean rag with one of the liquids and rub over the desired surface.

It may seen like you are removing some of the covering because it becomes sticky but all you are doing is activating a thin layer of the surface. It will dry and go back to its original state.

I have used acetone/lacquer thinner on some of the dirtiest fenders, lifelines, and shore power cords you could imagine. When I say the dirtiest, I mean some have been so black you could not tell what the original color had been. In every case, though, the acetone/lacquer thinner brought them back looking almost brand new.

(Note: Acetone/lacquer thinner will smear and erase names that are in ink on, for example, a plastic winch cover. Avoid going over the name).

Snaps

There is nothing more frustrating than fighting with a snap that is a million times smaller than yourself. On one particular boat, the snaps were so stubborn that when I went to unsnap the cover, the snaps stayed where they wanted, the material ripped out from around them, and I was sent sailing across the deck. I was so mad.

Do not wait until you notice the little darlings are becoming harder to unsnap before you do something about them because I can guarantee you they will at some point or another. Once a month, apply some petroleum jelly, such as, Vaseline or spray them with some WD-40. Doing so on a regular basis will help prevent corrosion and ward off potential tugs-of-war.

Stubborn Stains

Listed below are three of the most common stains found on a boat and how to eliminate them.

1. Water Run-Off. These stains occur most frequently in damp weather. The moisture in the air combines with any dirt that might be on the boat and runs down the sides. The constant flow of these two culprits leaves behind an ugly trail.

Do not pretend you do not see these stains. If the boat is made of wood, they will cause wood rot. If fiberglass be the case, they will become as fixed as the Rock of Gibraltar.

Try a cleaner/wax, such as Sea Powers, on these stains first. If that does not work, use a very fine rubbing compound. Be sure that the compound is the same color as the finish. For instance, you would not want to use a brown compound on a white surface. After compounding, go over the area with wax.

2. Rust Stains. Not only are these stains ugly, but they depreciate the value of a boat faster then any other maintenance problem -- unless, of course, you sink her.

Rust is the corrosion process of steel. It could be caused by impurities leaching from stainless steel, from hard water particles building up in one area (this is seen a lot around the bases of stanchions), from metal tools being left on the deck, and, perhaps, from someone cleaning their rigging with steel wool and the steel particles float to the decks of neighboring boats.

Rust begins as a light brown spot. Remove it immediately. Do not wait until it is a "cannot-ignore-it-orange."

There are a lot of good rust removing products on the market. If the rust stains are caught at an early stage, most commercial products will work. If the rust, however, has been overlooked for a prolonged period, more drastic measures may need to be taken. Listed below are some suggestions that have always worked well for me.

(**A word of caution:** The following products are very strong. Wear gloves and glasses. Keep the chemicals away from your face. Contain the substances to rusted areas only. If any of these chemicals get on any other surface of your boat -- for instance, if one starts running down the side of the boat -- wash it off immediately with detergent and water. Read manufacturer's

*Lubricating snaps on a regular basis
will ward off potential tug-of-war matches.*

labels from start to finish. Do your best to prevent any of these chemicals from going into the bay or down your driveway).

Muriatic Acid. I have discussed using this chemical earlier on rusted stainless steel and because the chemical is so powerful it warrants repeating how to use it on all rusted surfaces. Test a small, inconspicuous area of your boat first so you are sure the acid will not ruin the boat's finish.

Dry the rusted area. Keep a dry rag at your side for unexpected drips. With a small throw-away brush, dip the bristles directly into the container the acid comes in and paint over the rust. If the rust does not disappear before your eyes, it means that the rust has been neglected for too long and has permanently stained the finish.

Lime Away. (Test an inconspicuous area first for safety). Lime Away can be found in most grocery stores. Purchase the spray form. Spray Lime Away on the rusted area only. Let it penetrate for two or three minutes then wash it off with detergent and water.

Navel Jelly. You can buy Navel Jelly in any hardware store. It is a slower working chemical compared to the products already mentioned but it gets the job done, nonetheless. Follow the manufacturer's directions.

3. Transom Exhaust Stains. If you wash the transom with detergent and water after each use, you should never experience exhaust stains. If you are faced with a discolored transom, here are two of the most common types of stains and their solutions.

Rust Colored. Fill a plastic spray bottle halfway with muriatic acid and the other half with fresh water. Because acid has a tendency to soften paint, spray the solution on an unseen area first to test it. When you are **sure** it will not harm the finish, spray the stained area lightly. The rusted exhaust stain should disappear. Flush the area with plenty of detergent and fresh water. After the transom has dried, re-wax it.

Black Soot. Try detergent, fresh water, and plenty of elbow grease first. If that does not work, a fine rubbing compound should. Remember to buy a compound that is the same color as the boat's finish. Soot contains solvents that will dissolve wax. Re-wax when the stain is gone.

A good running diesel engine normally burns clean and will not leave behind a horrible reminder that the boat has been taken out. If you are having problems with discoloration, you might want to check the engine.

*Coiling your dock line is an important safety feature
and looks nice and nautical, too.*

Stain Prevention

Because oxidation and moisture help stains to develop, keep your boat clean, dry, and waxed.

Topside Scuffs

These marks, usually black, are nothing more than terrible eye sores. They are caused when the boat hits the side of the dock as it comes into its haven.

Acetone/lacquer thinner work great on these monsters. Make sure you re-wax after removing the spots.

To help preserve the topsides and the dock, "dock wheels" are recommended. (For the novice boat owner, we will call them "training wheels.") Keep the wheels clean with acetone or lacquer thinner.

Dock Lines

Part of your monthly detailing duties should be checking the dock lines for the following:

1. Worn out lines. For security reasons, replace lines that are wearing. Do not wait until the Harbor Patrol calls you to let you know your boat is floating away.

2. Tension. If dock lines are drawn too tight, they will snap.

3. Coiled dock lines. It is not only a safety precaution to coil your dock lines (people have a tendency to trip over dock line that is left in a heap) but it looks nice and nautical, too. (See the illustration on the previous page).

Shoes

Any shoes worn on the deck of a boat should have white soles with very small grooves in them.

Hence, shoes with dark soles leave hard-to-clean marks on the deck. And, shoes with deep grooves, more often than not, collect dirt particles which will scratch the finish. (Some "boat shoes" are the worst offenders).

Give a Darn and Lend an Arm

You might ask what water pollution has to do with the cosmetic aspects of your boat but, in my opinion, it has everything to do with it, for two reasons.

First, pollutants in the water will damage your perfectly-manicured

Give a darn - Lend an arm.

topsides. Whether it be diesel fuel staining them or a hard glass bottle denting them, it will happen.

Second, your boat just might be beautiful enough to blind you from the garbage and contaminating liquids you so often sail or power through. But, I can guarantee you the day you are told you cannot jump into the ocean to cool off or pull your child behind your boat to ski because the water is too contaminated, awareness of it all will be too late.

It is easy enough to start caring. Pick a piece of water and claim it as yours. Keep a fish net, or the like, in your boat and when you see some garbage float into your space, fish it out. I am not saying you have to do it every day. Add it to your detailing list. As for grease and the like, if you see where it is coming from, report it to the proper authorities.

Is taking five minutes every once and a while to help keep our magnanimous marine environment healthy, so much to ask?

I think not.

CHAPTER 4

TEAK TIPS

Sher's definition of teak wood:
"The only wood that can be left unprotected
against a harsh marine environment
and still weather the storm."

Throughout the boat building industry, when it comes time to select a wood for laying the decks, attaching the trim, and securing the handrails, teak wood has the best qualities for the job. Unlike ash, oak, and mahogany, teak contains a natural oil which makes it virtually rot proof. Teak has a high tolerance for an abusive marine environment and is pleasing to look at, even with age.

Teak wood has so many fine characteristics that you may think it is heaven sent. Well, it is not. It is imported from the Far East, having floated down many a great river and flown across foreign skies to finally serve your needs. But, even though teak is tough and readily available to serve your needs, it will last longer and look better if you give it some tender loving care whether you leave it natural or apply a dressing to it. Teak will survive either way, it is entirely a personal preference.

Leaving Teak Bare

The first, and seemingly the easiest, method for maintaining teak is to leave it bare and let it weather naturally. When teak is young and first introduced into the marine environment it is yellowish-brown. If the wood is allowed to weather naturally, without applying any commercial oils or chemicals to it, the natural oils in the wood will oxidize and turn the surface a beautiful silvery buff.

Unfortunately, keeping this silver patina does not come without a price

-- keeping your boat in a near-perfect environment. For example, a boat that sits more than it sails, is kept covered more than uncovered, and has little foot traffic is a good candidate for this type of finish. It is vital to keep the teak clean.

Teak kept in such pampered surroundings need only receive an occasional (about once a week) scrubbing -- across its grain -- with a soft bristle brush and a mild biodegradable soap, such as Tide or Wisk, and plenty of fresh water. If you have access to saltwater, drench the decks with it. Saltwater to teak is what Clorox is to clothes, a wonderful bleaching agent.

If you maintain bare teak on a regular basis, you will find that sometimes it is hard to tell if the natural weathered teak is clean or dirty because of the silver tint. If you are not sure, wet the teak with fresh water. If it turns a golden-brown, it is clean. If it turns black, it is dirty.

A Bare Nightmare

There are extreme cases to leaving teak bare. For example, we were maintaining a 42-foot Spoiler with four different levels of teak decking. The owner preferred to leave the decks bare, even though he enjoyed entertaining on a regular basis.

What fun we had cleaning and bleaching those teak decks just before every party to eliminate the chip and dip stains from the party before.

It did not make sense to us that the owner chose to have his decks cleaned and bleached every week instead of having us put a dressing on them which would have saved him lots of money and decking.

We wonder to this day if that boat owner ever realized those potato chips cost him a fortune.

Bleaching Precautions

Any time you use unfamiliar chemicals on your boat, test an inconspicuous part of the boat first to make sure they will not harm the surface. Make sure the boat does not have any leaks below because if it does, the cleaning/bleaching products will ruin curtains and/or furniture. Take everything off the boat you can that might get ruined by the chemicals.

Bleaching Teak

Before we get into the how to's of bleaching teak, I feel it important to say that, for the most part, the two-part acid cleaners available to us today

*Keeping the environment off teak
will help to keep it in its natural, silvery buff.*

are not biodegradable and harm our sensitive marine environment.

Unfortunately, the ones that work the best are the worst offenders, such as Te-Ka A&B and the long-standing team of oxalic acid and trisodium phosphate. I was, however, thrilled to see that Star Brite, which is a teak cleaner and brightener, boasts on their bottle that their product is environmentally safe. In addition, the West Marine hardware stores have come out with a teak cleaner/brightener which is biodegradable. It is also my understanding that West Marine plans on coming out with a whole line of biodegradable cleaning supplies. West Marine is a fine hardware store and I would recommend if you have one near you to use them and their new biodegradable product line.

If you need to clean up your teak, please try to use biodegradable products first. If the teak is so bad you have to use drastic measures, like a harsh product, try to only do it once and, perhaps, plug up the scuppers and use a wet-dry vacuum to suck up the harsh product. (We have done that before). Also, if you do enjoy a cleaning product that is not biodegradable, drop a quick note off to the manufacturers asking them to research a way to make the product biodegradable. I believe that between consumer comments and government demands, there will come a day where most cleaning products will be biodegradable.

I have one more comment to make about harmful marine cleaners and then I will get off my podium: Do not use them at all. Remember when this country was having a water shortage and brown grass was the "in" thing to have even in the most prestigious neighborhoods? Well, if you are worried about what the neighbors think about your dirty swimstep, get them to leave theirs dirty, too. Begin a "Dirty Teak Club." I am not saying to leave it dirty forever. Get yourself some biodegradable teak cleaner and clean it up slowly and save some fish rather than quickly and kill some fish.

No doubt about it, bleaching teak is not good for the wood. Bleach strips the natural oils from the wood, eats away at the grain, and, tends to dry out the seam compound. But, cleaning and bleaching wood that has been stained or neglected for a long period of time is the only way to get teak back to a quality state. Therefore, it is important to perform the cleaning and bleaching process as little as possible.

If your boat is used more for recreational purposes, such as fishing, houseboating, or water skiing, such things as food, suntan oil, and water and air pollution can turn that once silvery dream into a black nightmare.

Suddenly, the teak is stained black, the softer grain in the wood is wearing away, and, it is cracking and splitting.

Not only is the wood unsightly, but it can leave painful splinters in little and big fingers alike. Therefore, do not be like the boat owner previously mentioned. Unless you are able to keep your boat in a clean, dome-covered setting (or you like the looks of potato chip stained teak) protect and preserve the teak by first cleaning and bleaching it and then applying a dressing.

Of course, you *always* want to use the least caustic method when cleaning and bleaching your teak. So, from the examples below, pick the condition your teak is in and follow the recommendations. After the teak has dried, you will be applying a dressing to it. (Follow the directions on page 44, under *How and When to Apply*).

1. **Brand New or Close to It.** The teak's surface is smooth and uniform in color, either golden brown or weathered silver. The seam compound is perfectly intact.

If this be the case, and you are *sure* you want to go away from the legendary look of silver grace, scrub the wood with a soft bristle brush and some mild, biodegradable soap. Let the wood dry completely before you apply an oil to it. After cleaning, there should be no raised grain in wood in this good of shape. (Now, see *How and When to Apply* on page 44).

2. **Mediocre.** The grain in the wood is slightly raised. The color may be graying and, perhaps, there are a few spots from food, suntan oil, and the like. There could be some mildewed areas. Nevertheless, the seam compound is sound.

There is no cause for alarm here -- yet. You need not go to drastic measures to clean this wood. Visit your favorite marine hardware store and purchase some Star Brite or a comparable product. If there are no biodegradable products on the shelves, ask a clerk to recommend the least caustic products. After you have chosen a product, follow the directions on the back of the manufacturer's container. After the wood has dried completely and the color is uniform, sand the raised grain down smooth. You may have to use a coarse sandpaper first and work up to a finer one. When you have a clean, faired surface, either vacuum up the dust or wash it off, but make sure it is gone. Now, you are ready to apply your oil. (Follow the information on page 44, under the heading *How and When to Apply*) .

3. **Past the Point of No Return.** This teak is black and mildewed beyond recognition. The grain is raised to the point of towering over gullies

and valleys. The seam compound is cracking.

Teak this bad may seem like it does not have a chance for reincarnation, but I have seen the worst of the worst come back almost like new. It takes a grand effort to get it back there. Although I do not like to recommend Te-Ka A&B because it is not biodegradable, it is the only product that I know that gets right down into the fibers of the wood and lifts out the dirt and stains. My advice to you: Use this product once and put your teak on a good maintenance program so you do not have to use it again.

When using Te-Ka A&B, a lot of caution must be taken because it can be a very dangerous product. Read all the manufacturer's warnings and directions on the back. Also, do not use Te-Ka if your boat is painted -- it will ruin the paint. It also will ruin anodized aluminum. Either take the aluminum off the boat or wax the heck out of it and spray the chemicals off of it if any get on.

If you must use this chemical, try to schedule it on a cool day because if Part A dries out, it will stain the wood. Make sure that two people are working with the Te-Ka, one to scrub and one to keep the chemicals wet and off surrounding surfaces. Make sure both parties wear shoes and thick gloves. Te-Ka will do to your body what it does to the wood -- it literally eats it. My partner can give you testimony to that. Years ago, when we first started cleaning boats, my partner did not wear gloves. At the end of the day, she had huge holes in her knuckles. It was not, and is not, a funny situation.

In addition, before you start to use the product, soap down the boat real good or get the boat a plastic skirt which can be found in most marine hardware stores. To apply the chemicals, we generally use fingernail brushes. They are inexpensive and can be used over and over again. When you apply Part A, scrub it into the wood and do not let it dry out. Do not let it sit on the wood too long either. Maximum five minutes. You will need to rinse Part A off before you apply B. You will need lots of part B, the neutralizer. It is even a good idea to buy extra.

After you have finished cleaning and bleaching the teak, give the boat a good scrubbing with a mild detergent and soft bristle brush. Check all surfaces, waterways, and, especially the topsides for residue.

After the wood has dried, sand it down to a smooth surface and clean away the dust. (See *How and When to Apply* on page 44).

It must be noted here that if the seam compound is cracking and disappearing before your eyes, before you oil your decks, have a professional come out and take care of it for you -- unless, of course, you feel confident you can do it yourself.

Bleached To A Pulp

I want to share with you a story about a boat owner who believed totally in bleaching his teak until the day there was none left to bleach.

This boat owner went through boat detailing services like a change of clothes. When the old detailing crew got off his boat and the new got on, he would have them clean and bleach the teak. It was like a test they had to pass before they could maintain his boat. When it came around to being our turn to maintain his boat, the teak was so bad you could put a screwdriver through it. I refused to bleach his "pulp" and he just could not understand how it got that way. Needless to say, all the wood had to be replaced.

The moral of the story is: If you want healthy wood, bleach it as little as possible.

Teak Dressings

Teak dressings come in two forms: oils and sealers. The difference between the two is an oil penetrates deep into the wood, whereas a sealer remains on top. Both are quite effective. A sunscreen and an anti-fungus agent should be considered when purchasing either type.

The decision, however, to dress the teak is a far easier one to make compared to standing in front of rows of different teak dressings, mouth agape and clueless as to which one to buy. For this reason, I decided to compare the top seven dressings -- three oils and four sealers -- in the hope of helping the consumer before he or she pays a high price, applies the dressing, and then realizes that he or she does not care for the way the dressing leaves the teak.

Feeling like a cross between myself and David Horowitz, I based by study on color, ease of application, and finish. Here, then, are my results:

H.A. Calahan's Teak Oil. If you like the natural yellowish-brown color of teak, you will like this oil. Because Calahan's contains a sunscreen, it allows the surface to stay close to is original color. It also contains an anti-fungus agent and is easy to apply. It has a nice soft finish.

Mirror Glaze 46 Gold Teak Oil. This oil does just what the name implies. It leaves the teak with just a hint of gold to it. It is easy to apply and has a light golden finish.

First Mate Marine Teak Oil. Turns teak a burnt-orange color. It comes out of the can thick which might cause you to apply too much. Be careful of "globs." The finish is dark and somewhat dull.

Boat Life Teak Brite Sealer. This product has an "adult-proof" cap which is difficult to get off. Have a sharp pick or screwdriver handy. It turns teak a walnut-brown and darkens the grain. It is easy to apply, once you get the cap off! It has a warm finish to it.

Teak Wonder Sealer. This sealer leaves the teak rust-yellow in color. Application is easy, like applying rusted water. It contains silicones which would hinder varnish if you wanted to varnish the wood in the future. The finish is debatable.

Tip Top Teak Sealer. (Another "adult proof" cap). This sealer turns teak a cherry color. It is easy to apply. The finish has just a hint of a pleasant-red.

Watco Sealer. Gives teak a dark walnut tone. It is "sappy" to apply and care must be taken not to apply too much at one time. The finish is shiny and dense.

How and When to Apply

If you do not want your eyes to water and your head to ache for days, only apply dressings where there is plenty of ventilation. For example, do not apply dressings inside your garage. Years ago, I was oiling some teak in a hanger. The hanger was about 40-feet by 40-feet. It had a huge sliding door which, I thought, let in lots of air. I was wrong. I was oiling away when all of a sudden my eyes teared up and I could not see. I do not remember how I got off the boat but I made it outside to a fresh water faucet and flushed out my eyes. Luckily, there was no damage but it sure scared me.

To apply the dressing, I prefer to use a brush as opposed to a rag because a brush will not leave behind any lint or get caught on any snags that might be in the wood.

Watch for drips and wipe them up when they are wet because you will not be able to when they have dried.

How often should you apply oil? Here on the West Coast we clean the light surface dirt off the teak, let it dry and then apply the dressing about once a month. If you live in an area, however, where the ultra-violet rays are not as strong, or your boat is stored inside, you can wait as long as three to four months.

Steam Cleaning Teak?

Although I have searched for the perfect answer to this controversial subject, I did not find it. I have talked to professionals who had both good and bad to say about it. I have concluded that steam cleaning is quite harsh and could be detrimental to the teak. It should only be thought of as a last resort.

If there is something ingrained in the teak that you cannot get out by cleaning and bleaching, or through a water soluble paint/varnish remover, call a professional.

Check out the professional's references, ask questions, and for sure get a guarantee. **Do not try to do it yourself.**

Remember, Mother Nature has the final say.

CHAPTER 5
VARNISHING

Sher's definition of the art of varnishing:
"Enduring the tormenting details
so you can appreciate the beauty
that springs from your meticulous labors."

It is true: In waterfront taverns across the country, how to varnish is one of the most controversial subjects discussed among amateur and professional brightwork specialists alike. Indeed, a dozen methods are exchanged over a dozen sunsets, but never does one way of doing things rise from the rest and become the king of standards.

There are no absolutes, only fundamentals.

Varnishing is one of those skills anyone can acquire if he or she masters the fundamentals. Once the basics of brightwork are learned, you will develop your own style -- a way of doing things that works best for your personality.

This chapter contains the essentials of varnishing teak wood. (Woods such as oak, ash, and mahogany demand the use of different methods). **Do not** be in a hurry to learn and perfect these fundamentals. Perfection, remember, is the result of much time and practice. Whether professionals want to admit it or not, even they were awkward amateurs at one time or another.

Check the Weather Forecast

It is your time and sweat invested in producing a perfect varnished finish, but Mother Nature always determines what the final results will be.

For example, let us say the past two days have been bursting with perfect varnishing conditions. You have scraped and sanded happily (is that possible?) knowing the third day will bring the same wonderful conditions that will dry your varnish to a mirror finish. On the third day, however, as you are applying the final brush load of varnish, a threatening dark gray cloud hovers over your boat. You look up in disbelief. As raindrops start falling like little missiles on your unskimmed, tacky varnish, you know you are experiencing a harsh reality -- Mother Nature's punishment for not checking with her first.

To avoid unnecessary failures, on the morning you want to prepare or varnish a surface, listen to a local weather station for an up-to-date forecast. If you live close to the water, also do as my mentor, Bill Beck, did every morning before starting his day. He had a small dingy turned up side down in his backyard. If the dingy had dew on it, he knew it might not be the best of days to varnish. If the boat was dry, happily did he run out the door with paint and varnish in hand.

And, no, I am not saying a dingy is the best guide for moisture in the air. You can use just about anything -- the doghouse, the tops of cars, etc.

Ideal Weather Conditions

Overcast, dry air, temperature rising, no wind, and about 60 to 70 degrees. It is a good idea to varnish right after a rain storm because the air has been washed clean.

Unfavorable Weather Conditions

A sudden drop in temperature, rain, wind, and excessive heat. (How these conditions affect your varnish are discussed under the heading *Diseased Varnish* on page 64).

Do Not Get Caught With Your Varnish Down

When preparing a surface to receive a coat of varnish, only uncover what you can cover back up the same day. Do not leave bare wood exposed to the elements for any prolonged period of time.

Imagine how much exposed wood you would have if you spent a week stripping and sanding it. Now, assume the grand day comes when it is time to flow the first coat of varnish across that perfectly faired out surface and as you are pouring thinner into your varnish, the good Lord is pouring rain onto your prepared surface. You pack it in because you know you cannot varnish in the rain.

In the meantime, it pours rain for a week on your exposed wood. The weather has gotten under its smooth surface and has ripped out the soft grain. Dirt and mildew have formed, darkening the wood. Knowing you cannot varnish over mildewed, sandblasted wood, you fall to the deck of your boat with ego deflated and defeated. The truth hurts. You have got to start over!

What Condition is the Varnish In?

Listed below are three conditions typical of a varnished surface. The fourth situation, however, is wood that has been oiled, but is now under consideration for varnish. Read these descriptions and determine which category your varnished or oiled wood falls under. Follow the correct preparation method succeeding each interpretation.

1. Well-Maintained. The only imperfections in this varnish may be some nicks and/or dings which can be easily eliminated. The surface may be slightly dulled, an indication it needs a coat of varnish.

Surface Preparation: #220-Grit Method on pages 51 and 54.

2. Salvageable. This varnished finish has a lot of flaws, but can still be salvaged. The surface is dull and yellowing with, perhaps, some black spots and spidery lines breaking through it.

Surface Preparation: #60-Grit-Knockdown Method on page 54.

3. Has To Be Stripped. Time, neglect and the ultraviolet rays of the sun have christened this varnish, "Beyond Repair." It is lusterless, monacing looking, and harmful to the eyes. The only thing paying any attention to it now is the weather.

Surface Preparation: Varnish Stripping Methods on pages 54 - 57.

4. From Oil to Varnish. Yes, you can switch from oil to varnish. The important question is, "Did the teak dressing you were using contain silicones?" If so, the silicones will react to the newly applied varnish like oil does to vinegar -- they just do not mix and the varnish will not adhere to the wood.

But it can and has been done successfully many times before. The key to success in this situation is to use a powerful cleaning and bleaching agent, such as Teka, and to sand away a considerable amount of wood to get down to fresh stuff.

Surface Preparation: This surface needs to be cleaned and bleached. See *Bleaching Teak,* in Chapter 4, *Teak Tips.*

Sandpaper

For all the above surface preparations you will be using sandpaper. Please consider the following advice:

1. Purchase a good quality sandpaper that contains aluminum oxide. Keep your surface and paper dry. If the sandpaper gets wet and you continue sanding with it, you will create small, aluminum scratch-like lines in the surface of the wood. You will not notice them until it is too late. They will be smiling up at you through what you thought to be your best varnish job ever.

2. Wet or dry sandpaper? The biggest difference in these two papers is expense. The wet sandpaper is quite a bit more than the dry. But, the end results are the same in either case; both prepare the surface to receive the applied finish. The best time to use wet sandpaper is when there is a lot of dew in the air and on the surface and you know it will not burn off until later. Using wet sandpaper enables you to get the damp surface prepared in time to get a coat of varnish on whereas you could not with dry paper. Another great advantage to using wet sandpaper is that, because you are using water, you can see what your surface will look like with the next coat of varnish. If the water does not temporarily hide the flaws, the varnish will not permanently. (Also, wiping the surface with a thinner rag will show any imperfections). **Never prepare bare wood with wet sandpaper.**

Folding Sandpaper Effectively

Around the harbor, we could always pick out the amateur boat maintenance workers by the way they folded their sandpaper. Usually they had the paper folded in such a way that the rough edges rubbed against each other.

You want the sandpaper to work for you, not against you. It is really quite easy. Follow the instructions on pages 52 - 53. You should end up with a piece of sandpaper that is approximately 5 1/2 inches by 4 1/2 inches to work with. This size is excellent for large surfaces such as handrails, toerails, and bulkheads.

For smaller surfaces, such as small pieces of trim, take a quarter of a piece of sandpaper and follow the same folding instructions. This will give you better control of the paper which reduces the chances of scratching gelcoat or paint.

Hand Sanding Block/Electric Sander

Not only does using a sanding block or an electric sander give your hand a break from sanding, but they also produce a smoother surface. I recommend especially using these tools on large flat surfaces, leaving the smaller pieces of trim to be done by hand. I say this because I have seen a lot of damage caused by an electric sander.

Because of the speed of an electric sander, a young man thought he could save time (make more money) if he used the speedy sander on some small pieces of trim. He did so. Standing back to admire his work, he noticed he had added a new look to the boat: tiny swirl marks etched into the gelcoat, compliments of the speed sander.

Unfortunately, the young man really defeated his own purpose because it not only cost him more time, but it also cost him a lot more money -- a very expensive boo-boo.

Varnishing Preparation Methods

You might not appreciate this rule of thumb but **preparation is 99% of the finished product and, for the most part, the biggest pain in the neck.**

As much as you want to hurry through it, do not. Take your time and pay close attention to details. A clean, perfectly faired surface is going to give you a much better finish then a dirty, rough one.

Remember also to uncover only those surfaces that you can cover with varnish on the same day. My mentor, Bill Beck, has a fail safe method he uses religiously, unless Mother Nature has a mood swing. He prepares in the morning and washes down the prepared surfaces before he goes to lunch. When he returns, the surfaces are dry and ready for the varnish.

#220-Grit Method. This method is to be used to build up coats of varnish on an already mirror perfect surface, with the exception of a few nicks or dings.

1. Clean any nicks or dings with thinner. Lightly sand the imperfect areas with #220-grit sandpaper. Be careful not to expose the underlying wood.

2. Clean the sanded areas with thinner again and apply a coat of varnish only to the damaged areas. Keep applying coats of varnish until the damaged area becomes level with the surrounding finish. Make sure to let the varnish dry. Sand it between each new coat.

Folding Sandpaper Effectively.

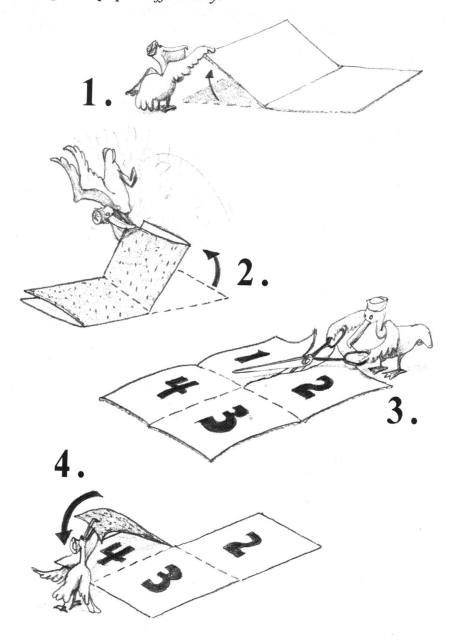

5.

6.

7.

Do not be a nerd . . . just follow the bird.

3. After bandaged areas are dry, sand the entire surface which is to receive the coat of varnish. This means you will be sanding over fixed areas again. Use #220-grit sandpaper to do so.

4. Because this varnish is in such good condition, you do not want to remove it. You only want to create "tooth" so the new varnish has something to stick to. The sanded surface should look like a sanded surface -- no shiny spots.

5. After sanding, see *Clearing the Decks* on page 58.

#60-Grit-Knock-Down Method. This technique is used to preserve a varnished finish one last time before it has to be completely stripped.

1. Yellow air pockets. These imperfections are mere voids in the varnish. Simply take a sharp razor blade, or pin, and poke a small hole in the top of the air pocket. When you flow your first coat of varnish across it, it will fill and disappear.

2. Black spots. These are blackened areas which have broken through the varnish. Clean the spots with thinner and sand with a #60-grit sandpaper. If the discoloration does not disappear with sanding, stop. Do not sand a hole in the wood so you have a crater to fill later. Instead, see *Bleaching Teak* instructions in Chapter 4, *Teak Tips*.

3. Wipe over the areas with thinner. Varnish just those areas mended. Keep adding coats until the spots are back up to the level of the surrounding finish. Be sure to let the varnish dry between coats and sand with 220-grit sandpaper.

4. When you have a dry, even surface, sand the entire area to be varnished with #60-grit sandpaper. You want to really "knock" that old varnish down to eliminate spidery lines and the dull finish.

5. Because the #60-grit sandpaper is so course, it will leave unwanted scratches in your finish. Sand the entire area again and use a finer sandpaper, such as #120-grit and finish with an even finer paper like #220-grit.

6. After sanding, see *Clearing the Decks* on page 58.

Varnish Stripping Methods

Listed below are three of the most common methods for stripping varnish. Find the style that works best for you and stick to it.

1. Dry Scraping. This method is the best to use on thick varnish and when you need to get under the surface of the wood. It is also the least expensive of the varnish stripping methods. However, it is more physically taxing. The tools you will need are a good hook scraper and a scraper file. It is imperative that you keep the scraper sharp because it could cause damage to the surface. You will know when the scraper is becoming dull because it seems to takeover. It will literally veer off course and leave a permanent smile in the wood as if to say, "Ha, Ha, Ha! I got you." One other thing that bears mentioning about sharpening scrappers -- **do not do it onboard!** The little metal flakes that so silently fall to the decks of boats come back later as roaring rust problems.

Like everything else in life, dry scraping takes practice to perfect. If you are a beginner, just take it slow. There really is only one standard way to operate a hook scraper. Simply hold the scraper at a right angle to the wood, bear down and pull the varnish toward you. Do not bear down to the left or right. Keep pulling straight.

2. Paint/Vanish Removers. Most of these types of chemicals are very powerful. Wear gloves and protective eyewear. And, although I have never felt any side affects from breathing in the chemical (I have always used this sort of product out in the open air of some Southern California harbor) it is good thinking to wear some sort of air-supplied respirator or vapor mask. Stripping varnish would not be worth losing any vital body functions.

Because chemical removers will weaken gelcoat and paint, try to remove the piece you want to strip from the boat. If that is impossible and the chemical remover lands in forbidden territory, rinse if off immediately.

Apply your first coat of remover to the area you wish to strip using an inexpensive bristle brush. After the chemical stops bubbling, *leave it on* and apply a second coat. Wait until this coat stops bubbling and check to see if there are any yellow or orange blotches looking up at you through the goo. If there are, keep applying the chemical until they go away. Once the bubbling has ceased and there are no patches of orange or yellow, you can remove it. To do this, get yourself a sharp putty knife and remove the lifted varnish, being extremely careful not to gouge the wood. Put the waste into a contianer that can be sealed and disposed of properly. *Properly* does not mean in the marina's dock box or in your garbage can at home. Call your local environmental agency and ask what to do with it. *Please.*

After you have removed the chemical, scrub the stripped pieces with a soft bristle brush, detergent, and fresh water. If you have used the chemical remover on a boat, make sure you give the boat a good washing down, paying particular attention to the topsides.

When stripping is complete and all traces of the chemical have been washed from nooks and crannies, the wood should then be cleaned, bleached, and sanded. (See *Bleaching Teak* in Chapter 4, *Teak Tips).*

3. The Heat Gun Method. I like this method the best because it is faster than dry scraping and not as messy as the chemical removers. If you chose this method of stripping, you will need:

☐   A heat gun

☐   A sharp scraper

☐   A scraper file

☐   A dust mask

☐   A vacuum cleaner

☐   A strong back

First, before you begin your project, make sure your scraper is sharp. Again, if you are working on a boat, go somewhere downwind and, also, away from any neighboring boats. I would like to mention here, too, that when you consider purchasing a scraping partner for your heat gun, do not buy one with a plastic handle. That might sound like common sense to you but sometimes it does not hit home to some of us until it is too late.

For example, when I did my first job with a heating gun, I supplied my entire crew with scrapers sporting plastics handles. The handles were so hot to work with, they took me off their Christmas list that year

The most important thing to remember about using a heat gun is that it will lift paint, break glass, and soften gelcoat. Therefore, if it is not possible to keep the heat away from these vulnerable areas, attach a batten (a thin piece of wood) to the area you want to protect.

The process of the heat gun method is very simple. The heat from the heat gun softens the varnish and the scraper pulls it from the surface. Using both the heat gun and scraper in unison will take practice.

To begin, aim the heat gun at the area you wish to strip. Do not keep the heat on one area for any longer than five to seven seconds or until the area starts to bubble. It is common for the beginner to burn through the varnish into the wood because they do not pay close attention to what the varnish is doing.

Once the varnish has softened, use your scraper and pull the melted varnish toward you, working at all times with the grain of the wood, not against it. With practice, you will be able to work the heat gun just ahead of the scraper at the same time and speed.

In addition, I recommend that you clean as you go, either with a vacuum cleaner or broom and dust pan. There are a few reasons for this. First, when the melted varnish dries and hits the ground, it has a tendency to catch fire. Second, varnish residue is not biodegradable and not something you want showing up on your dinner table later as you are cutting into the catch of the day. Finally, you do not want to track the varnish flakes into the cabin of the boat or your house.

After the surface has been stripped of varnish, there likely will be old varnish and fillers embedded in the pores of the wood. Do not try to get at them with your scraper. Instead, you can do one of two things:

You can leave the wood as is and use the ingrained varnish as a filler coat. I have seen this method used successfully. Simply sand over the areas you want to varnish with an #80-grit sandpaper and follow up with finer grits until you have a perfectly smooth surface. The important thing to remember if you want to do this is to check the wood for discoloration. Normally, sanding down and then revarnishing only works if the varnish is fairly new. After you finish sanding, you can revarnish.

You likely will need to use a chemical stripper on the surfaces to remove the old varnish and fillers. Follow the directions on pages 55 - 56. After using the chemical stripper, clean and bleach the wood to bring it back to a clean uniform color, follow directions on pages 38 - 42. After the wood has dried completely, begin with a coarse sandpaper and end your sanding project with a finer number, such as #220-grit. You want the wood to be smooth and uniform in color throughout. Now, you can either oil or revarnish the newly restored wood.

Clearing the Decks

The surface prepared, all that is left to do now is clear the decks and make way for the varnish!

To begin, take an abrasive pad, such as a 3M ScotchBrite pad, and some fresh water and scrub down the sanded surfaces. Using the abrasive pad ensures cleanliness and adds an extra "tooth" to the surface so that the varnish has something more to cling to.

While you are washing down the surfaces, pay close attention to what they look like wet. For example, are the yellow air pockets and bandaged areas disappearing when wet? If not, they will not when varnished. This is your last chance to fix those areas.

After you are sure the surface is clean, hose off the surrounding areas. You do not want any dust around that might get stirred up later and land in your varnish. You have worked too hard for that to happen.

Some professional varnishers use a vacuum to clean up as opposed to water. This is a good method to use if you are in an area where the water would not dry in time to get a coat of varnish on in the same day.

After your surface is clean, take a break. When you get back, the surface should be clean and dry and ready for a coat of varnish.

It is true: If you have been meticulous in preparing the surfaces to receive a coat of varnish, and you are just as careful when you apply it, you will be pleased with the results.

Varnishing Checklist

☐ Ideal Weather Conditions

☐ A Drop Cloth

☐ A Tack Rag

☐ Masking Tape

☐ Proper Thinner to Conform to Weather

☐ Varnish

☐ Brushes

☐ Clean Containers

☐ Clean Cotton Rags

☐ Sharp Razor Blade or Pin

☐ Stick-to-itiveness

To Mask or Not to Mask?

I know of a few brightwork specialists who can really cut a fine line with their varnishing brushes and do not need to use masking tape on any of the boat's surfaces. I recommend, especially if you are just a beginner, that masking be done.

When choosing a masking tape, I can guarantee you will not find anything better then the 3M brands and they make quite a number of them. If you purchase a simple painter's quality masking tape, **make sure** you do not leave it on the boat overnight. You will be sorry if you do. I have run across boats that boast tape residue all over themselves even though the tape had been removed months prior but had been left on for more then a day. The best masking tape to buy is the bright, lime-green stuff because you do not have to remove it the same day you put it on. Products, however, differ somewhat across the country and I would say that if this green, heaven-sent tape is not sitting in your local hardware store, ask questions about your options. That is what the people working behind those counters are there for.

When you have found the tape you want to use, mask off the areas you will be varnishing that day. I have seen people mask off their work area in different ways. For example, because varnish does not run up a surface, some people simply mask off the underside of the teak, where the teak meets the gelcoat or paint. This method should only be used by the sure-of hand. I would suggest that if you are a novice, you tape off both the bottom and the top just in case you goof. When laying your tape, give a little bit of breathing room between the wood and the adjoining surface, whether it be wood or gelcoat. Doing this will ensure that the varnish seals with the surface and, also, that when you take the tape off, you are only peeling up the tape and not your new varnishing job.

Are Your Rags Good Enough?

It is important that you prevent all rags from touching a prepared surface unless you know where they have been. For example, if a rag was used for dusting the interior or waxing the topsides, it will be contaminated with traces of oil and wax. Rags such as these, used on a freshly prepared, surface will prevent the varnish from sticking to it.

Buying Brushes

Whether you purchase a polyfoam disposable brush or a top of the line bristle brush such as Badger is entirely up to you. For the most part, both brushes produce the same results. The nicest quality about the disposable brushes is at the end of a long day, you simply throw them away as opposed to spending an hour on clean up. If you do use disposable brushes, however, I hope you are disposing of them properly. Make the effort, if not. If, on the other hand, you want to use a bristle brush, do yourself a favor and fork out a little more money for a more expensive brand. The cheaper bristle brushes tend to shed in wet varnish, which does not make for a good time.

Preparing Brushes

If you are using a polyfoam brush, check it for unwanted hitchhikers, such as lint or a friendly gnat, and whisk them away. If you are using a bristle brush, submerge the bristles in thinner and spin the handle between your palms and fingers. Do this in a container so that the thinner, and whatever is clinging to it, does not go all over the boat. Do this procedure two or three times.

Quit Eyeballing That Can!

If you have the urge to varnish out of the manufacturer's can, do not. Doing so will only contaminate the varnish. Instead, use paper buckets, which can be found in any marine hardware store, although keep your eye on them. After a few hours of use, the paper buckets tend to soften around the bottom and become moist. Whatever surface the bucket was sitting on will be branded.

Better, use clean, empty soup cans, or the like. Try to use cans that will accommodate your brush size. **Stay away from glass jars of any kind.** Breaking one on the boat, dock, or driveway could be quite dangerous.

Pour just enough varnish in the container to get you from point A to point B. This will keep the varnish clean and prevent needless waste. Once you pour the varnish out of the manufacturer's can, you should never pour it back in, unless, you do it all in the same motion.

Thinning Varnish to Conform to the Weather

Think of the weather and varnish in terms of a one-sided marriage. The weather is set in her ways and unwilling to change. The varnish must conform to her moods if the marriage is going to work.

When needed, we help the varnish agree with his partner by adding a particular thinner to it. Most marine manufacturers produce slow and fast thinners for different brushing and weather conditions. For example, Z-Spar makes numbered thinners. The higher the number on the front of the can, the slower the thinners curing time will be; the lower the number the faster the thinner will cure -- dry and harden -- the varnish.

In the summer, when temperatures are warmer, you will want to use a higher numbered thinner, such as the T-11, to slow down the varnish's drying time. If you do not slow it down, it will dry too fast, not flow properly, and lap marks will appear.

When temperatures are cooler, you will want to use a lower numbered thinner, such as the T-8. This thinner will set the varnish off quick and get it well on its way to drying before you lose the warmest part of the day.

How Much Thinner?

Because you want the first coat of varnish to penetrate deep into the wood, the formula should be one-quarter thinner to three-quarters varnish.

For additional coats, the varnish should be the same consistency as when it **first** came out of the manufacturer's can. When you notice the varnish thickening or your brush dragging, add about a teaspoon of thinner and stir *gently* -- so gently as to not create bubbles.

Filling Your Brush

1. Polyfoam. Submerge the sponge halfway into the varnish. It will fill quickly. On the count of three, pull the brush out.

2. Bristle Brush. Dip the bristles one-third to one-half their length into the varnish. Any excess should be eliminated by tapping the bristles against the side of the container. Do not drag them across the top. Doing so will ruin their natural shape.

Flow a Coat

Stop where you are! Before you flow that coat of varnish, take a tack rag and go over the prepared surfaces. Varnish should flow across a prepared surface like molasses on a sheet of glass. With this in mind, flow on about four inches of varnish using light even strokes in all directions to ensure absorption into the pores. End with strokes going in one direction with the grain. Do not overwork the varnish. The less you brush, the better the results.

Start again a few inches away from the wet patch and work back toward it. You should always be pulling your brush into the wet varnish, not away from it. Continue in this manner. (See the illustration on page 63).

Do not put a lot of pressure on the brush. You want the brush to barely touch the surface. The varnish should separate the brush from the surface at all times.

If you find the brush dragging, the varnish is too thick or you are not using enough of it. If the varnish drips, you are either using too much or it is too thin.

If your brush is becoming sticky, your hands probably are, too. Take a minute and clean up. This will prevent the varnish from running down your arm and you will feel better after a break.

Flying Objects

If you notice a bug take a nose dive into your wet varnish, as hard as it might be not to pick it out, ignore it. Saving its life is not worth ruining your finish.

When the varnish dries, brush away what remains of the unfortunate bug with a soft cotton rag. Its little paw prints will barely be noticeable. This also goes for dust particles and the like.

On the other hand, if the problem is an innocent bystander's hand print, you may as well have them date and sign it because it is there until you have time to sand it out.

Drying Time Between Coats

No matter where you live, your varnished surface should cure the same day you put it on so that the next day you can add another coat if need be. The best thing to do if you are not sure it is cured by the end of the day is

Working into the wet will be your best bet.

to test it. In the least conspicuous area, lightly scratch the surface of the varnish. If some comes off, it is not cured. You will more then likely have to revarnish it. Often varnish does not have the opportunity to cure because it is applied too late in the afternoon. The temperature is dropping and the following morning you are greeted with a flat, sticky finish.

How Many Coats?

From the list below, find the surface preparation method you performed and apply the number of coats recommended.

Method	*Coats*
#220-Grit Method	1
#60-Grit Knock-Down Method	3
Varnish Stripping Method	9

After these essential coats are applied, flow a coat of varnish every three months. **Do not wait until your varnish starts looking diseased!**

If you keep your varnish covered, however, which is the wise thing to do, I might add, you can go as long as a year without adding a coat. (See *Maintaining Varnish: Enemy Overboard* in Chapter 2).

Storing Varnish

At the end of the day, **do not pour used varnish back into the manufacturer's can!** If you do, it will contaminate the fresh varnish. Instead, dispose of the used varnish properly. The fresh varnish still in the can should be stored properly. After varnish has been opened, its nature is to form a skin over the top which makes it difficult to work with. To eliminate this problem, seal the lid tightly so no air can get in and store the can upside down. The next time you use the varnish, the skin will be on the bottom, not on the top.

Diseased Varnish

Before you bring the boat doctor down to see your sick varnish, see if you can diagnose the problem yourself by using the list below:

Alligatoring. Remember Aunt Ruth's alligator bag? This condition is usually brought on by the puddling of thick varnish.

Black Spots. Looks like the varnish has dark patches of wood warts. They

*Keeping your varnish on a healthy maintenance program
will prevent the aches, pains and
expense brought on by the boat doctor.*

are caused by dirt and/or mildew penetrating the varnish and soiling the underlying wood.

Blistering. Varnish seems to have an acne problem. This condition can be caused by excessive heat either during the application or right after the varnish has been applied. Blisters may also appear if the surface is too warm. Blisters may appear due to moisture trapped beneath the varnish or a foreign substance seeping from the wood.

Blooming. The fog has rolled in to stay on your freshly varnished surface. The causes for this clouding can be: varnishing to late in the day when the heat is dropping and the dew level is rising, or extreme humidity.

Brush marks. You would think Picasso had spent the night on your boat. These marks are left by working the varnish too much, or the varnish skinning over before it had a chance to flow out evenly.

Cracking. This varnish is like dry skin that begins to crack open. This condition is due to the varnish being thick, old, and weathered.

Curtains. This varnish looks like the person who lost all the weight, but not the flab. Too much varnish was used or it was too thick when it was applied.

Flat. Varnish with anemia which lacks its full luster. This is what happens when temperatures drop before the varnish has had a chance to skim over.

Grittiness. Looks like the nonskid on the deck of a boat. Dirty methods and brushes used during application cause this problem.

Holidays. Small (hopefully) areas missed in the varnished surface that remind the perfectionists that even they are not beyond error.

Nicks and Dings. Battle wounds that can be easily mended. These tragedies usually occur on the weekends when you invite your non-boating friend, Mr. Landlubber, for a Sunday bay cruise. In his excitement, Mr. Landlubber slams his six-pack down on your varnished caprail.

Runs. Looks like the varnish has shed a tear here and there.

This misfortune is due to applying too much varnish at one time, not brushing it out, and/or sloppy work habits.

Spidery Lines. The varnish looks like a spider "webbed" all over it. This problem is caused by over exposure to the weather.

Yellow-Air-Pockets. Imprisoned air bubbles that held their breath so long that their little faces turned yellow. This is caused by some type of trauma to the varnished surface.

Your Rights

When it comes to a wet, varnished surface, you have the right-of-way. For example, if you are varnishing on a boat and the guy next to you decides he wants to do some sanding, you have the right to tell him to stop. If you do not, his dust particles may end up in your wet varnish and destroy the finish. If he is a jerk about it and sands anyway, he is responsible for any damage he may have caused.

This principle of etiquette reminds me of one summer when my mentor, Bill Beck, and I were varnishing on two separate boats. As we were laying down fresh coats of varnish, the guys in the boat yard next to us began grinding away on their sanders. Because we were downwind, the dust particles began settling nicely into our fresh varnish.

Bill immediately asked them to stop. I remember thinking that that big boat yard of thirty workers was not going to stop production for a pair of insignificant boat maintenance people. I just knew a fight was going to ensue. But, to my surprise, they did stop.

Hiring a Professional

The best advice I can give when looking for a professional to work on your boat is to ask a neighboring boat owner, or the manager of your favorite marine hardware store. Word of mouth is most often the best advertisement.

I know of a boat owner who really got stung because he did not do his homework before hiring a "here-in-the-summer, gone-in-the-winter" young person.

Fly-by-night, told the boat owner that he needed to be paid half the amount being charged before he could start the job. In blind faith, the boat owner gave him about five-hundred dollars.

The boat was never touched.

Cover It Up!

Whether you have just read this chapter or you have already physically experienced the joys and pains of varnishing, you are aware of the time and money involved in obtaining a quality finish.

Knowing this, then, why would you not cover it up? You would not let a sea gull dump all over your Waterford crystal, would you?

	THE VARNISHING DO NOT FORGET LIST
SPRING	
SUMMER	
FALL	
WINTER	

THE TEN COMMANDMENTS
OF VARNISHING

1. Check The Weather Forecast

2. Mother Nature Has The Final Say

3. Do Not Get Caught With
   Your Varnish Down

4. Pay Close Attention To Details

5. Preparation Is 99% Of The Finished Product

6. Practice Clean Work Habits

7. Thin Varnish To Conform To The Weather

8. Always Layoff Into The Wet

9. Flow A Coat *Before*
   The Varnish Looks Diseased

10. Cover It Up!

CHAPTER 6

COMPOUNDING, WAXING, AND REPAIRING GELCOAT

Sher's definition of compounding and waxing:
"An endless, grueling game called 'Shine and shield.'
The object of the game is to keep the sun's destructive clutches from
making chalk out of the boat's gelcoat."

There is a misconception floating about the boating industry that fiberglass gelcoat is maintenance free. Perhaps this myth has been brought on by ambitious boat-builders and over-zealous sales pitches?

But the truth of the matter is gelcoat, like the paint on a car, will begin to fade and breakdown if it is not properly maintained. So, right now, tie an anchor to the misconception that gelcoat is maintenance free and let it sink to the bottom of the ocean where it belongs. Rest assured, if you are ignoring your boat's gelcoat, the sun is reducing it to powder.

Most often boat owners do not realize they have been neglecting their gelcoat until after a relaxing harbor cruise. As they are getting off their boat, they look down at their most cherished boating outfit and realize there is more gelcoat on their clothes than on the boat.

Do not be a gelcoat abuser. It just is not wise to ignore a one-thousandth of an inch coat of resin whose only purpose in life is to keep your boat afloat. Once the gelcoat is gone, it is gone for good.

That Magical Fiberglass Armor
Before we talk about maintaining gelcoat, it is important to understand exactly what fiberglass gelcoat is and why maintaining

it is so crucial to the integrity of your boat.

Fiberglass gelcoat is a thin coat -- about one-thousandth of an inch -- of unsaturated polyester resin which is sprayed into the female molds before the underlying fiberglass/polyester laminates are layed up. The gelcoat protects the fiberglass from weathering and abrading. If the gelcoat is not maintained it becomes porous, allowing water to seep into the matrix of the foundational fiberglass. If moisture is allowed to rest inside the laminates for a long period of time, the gelcoat will take on a dull, blotchy look. Neglected gelcoat becomes a permanent home to stubborn stains and runs down the value of your boat.

Wash-Downs

Wash-downs are the most effective way to maintain the integrity of your boat's gelcoat.

Washing down your boat periodically -- definitely after each use -- removes gritty particles (salt, sand and scum) from the surface of the gelcoat. When wash-downs are not preformed, these gritty culprits rub against the gelcoat and begin to break it down.

We help the breakdown process by wearing shoes with grooves in them where particles get stuck. When we walk around on the deck of the boat, we are scratching away at the gelcoat.

When we do not wash down, and we fender our boats to a dock, the fenders grind the salt, sand, and scum into the side of the boat. A clue that this is happening is discoloration in the gelcoat.

Wash-downs are simple and well worth the few minutes they take. Granted, the last thing one wants to do after spending the day out in the sun and excitement is wash the boat. You are just too tired, I know. But, an extra effort at the end of the day will ensure many more days of fun in the sun.

It is important to note here that it is a good idea to dry your boat after the wash-down to eliminate hard water build-up, especially if you are not using soft water. Adding a liquid wash/wax to your wash-down water will help to preserve any wax finish. (For more details on wash-downs, see Chapter 2 *Wash-Downs*).

Compounding

Whether gelcoat is in good shape or bad, it must always be compounded before it is waxed. Ultraviolet rays from the sun cause the pigments in the gelcoat to fade. In darker gelcoat colors, such as blue and red, the fading is more evident than in lighter colors.

The rate at which the fading occurs depends upon the grade of the gelcoat. Boat manufacturers use different grades. If you are interested in the quality of gelcoat on your boat, you can contact the manufacturer who should be happy to help you.

All grades need to be compounded before they are waxed to remove all the faded pigment. If not, your boat could end up like this poor fellow's:

A friend of mine, Chuck Reed, whose forte is compounding and waxing fiberglass boats, told me of a time he gave a bid on a job, but lost it to a kid who under bid him by about two-thousand dollars. (The boat, from what I understand, had been sitting in the sun for years without maintenance of any kind. It was a mess).

What Chuck and his crew would have done in two weeks, the young hustler did in a day.

The boat looked good for about a week. But, by the end of the seventh day, the gelcoat was dull again with huge flat streaks running through it where the oxidation, that should have been removed in the first place, bled through the wax.

Unfortunately, the boat owner who thought he was getting a good deal got ripped off instead. All the kid did was saturate the oxidation with some wax which made the gelcoat look wet for a short time. You could get the same effect by putting water on a sanded surface. It looks great when it is wet, but when it dries it looks the same, if not worse.

I have seen different methods used around the harbor and young Mr. Hustler's is definitely not one I recommend.

In addition to making sure you compound before you wax your boat, it is important to understand that when you are applying the compound, the compound is removing a micro-thin layer of gelcoat, leaving you with a clean surface to apply wax to.

Using the descriptions that follow, determine to what degree the surface of the gelcoat has deteriorated, if at all, and use the compounding method that best fits your situation.

Keep in mind that the worse it is, the harsher your products will have to be to clean it up. Because the sun will make the job more miserable than

The answer is simple:
Using soft cotton rags on gelcoat that
is only one-thousandth of an inch thick will ensure longer life
than taking a harsh polishing machine to it.

it already is, move the boat into some shade. If moving it is not possible, I suggest an early start.

Pristine. Since day one, this gelcoat has been kept cleaned and waxed on a regular basis, keeping the sun from starting its deterioration process. Because this gelcoat is in such good shape, it is only necessary to use a fiberglass cleaner/wax on it. Sea Power puts out an excellent cleaner/wax for just this surface type.

The cleaner/wax contains a fine rubbing compound, which cleans the surface, and a thin coat of wax to seal it. Apply the substance to the surface using a soft cotton rag and take it off in the same fashion. Gelcoat this good has never known trauma. Do not start by taking a machine to it.

Just a Hint. This is the gelcoat that does not get any attention until it starts to show signs of deterioration. The boat owner usually waits until he or she sees a chalk-like substance developing over the resin. Unfortunately, waiting for the ''hint'' only means more of the gelcoat has to be taken off to get a clean surface.

To clean up this gelcoat, use a paste fiberglass rubbing compound. Boat Armour and Dupont both make excellent products. These compounds are gritty and will remove the faded pigment to get to some new gelcoat. Some professionals mix a cleaner/wax with the compound for moisture which makes the substance easier to work with.

Compounds have a tendency to dry quickly and become quite difficult to remove.

Working the compound into the gelcoat can be done in two ways. It can be applied with a soft, white Scotch-Brite pad by 3M which comes attached to a handle. 3M makes different colored pads. Make sure for compounding purposes that you use only the white one. The other colors are much too coarse and will scratch the gelcoat surface.

Or, you can apply the compound with a power polisher with a nylon buffing pad. If you choose this method, be very careful. Keep in mind that the gelcoat layer is very thin. A machine removes a lot of gelcoat at one time and could go right through to the fiberglass. A machine also leaves tiny swirl marks if not handled properly. I suggest that if you are not familiar with running a machine that you seek the advice and/or assistance of a professional.

When compounding is complete, apply a hard paste fiberglass wax.

(See Waxing below).

Used-to-be-Gelcoat. The only thing that remains of this gelcoat is chalk. The pigment should be sent on its way to gelcoat heaven.

Usually, removing gelcoat that is this bad takes an extreme measure such as wet and dry sanding. If this be the case, it can only work once because so much gelcoat has to be removed that it should never be done again. If a shiny surface can be obtained, and with proper maintenance, it could last for a few more years. Otherwise, the surface will have to be painted.

So, whether you are the boat owner or the maintenance person of a boat in this condition, a professional should be consulted. I am not saying you cannot do it yourself, but have someone with a trained eye tell you exactly what you should do about the problem.

Waxing

After compounding, the gelcoat is left unprotected against the elements of a harsh marine environment and up for grabs. Applying a wax to the gelcoat is like appointing it its very own bodyguard. Not only will the wax keep undesirable matter from the gelcoat, but the coat of wax absorbs microscopic scratches, etc., which would otherwise be taken in by the gelcoat. The best kind of wax to use on gelcoat is a hard paste carnuba wax with an ultraviolet screen. *Fiberglass* wax usually is chock-full of ultraviolet filter additives. The most important thing to remember when purchasing a wax for your boat is to *make sure* that the wax is made specifically for boats and *not for* cars. The reason for this is an obvious one: The chemists creating boat waxes clearly understand the difference between the polyester resins which make up gelcoat as opposed to the lacquer finishes found on cars.

As for the application, apply and take off the wax by hand using soft cotton rags. Yes, you can use a machine but I just do not believe in using machines unless you need to remove a thin layer of gelcoat -- or, unless you have the skills to run one. I have acquired this attitude against machines because of all the damage I have seen caused by their misuse.

I think the biggest reason people choose to use a machine versus cotton rags is that they think a machine is faster and easier. Let me dispel that myth right now. Believe me, it is just as grueling to hold a machine in your arms for hours as it is to work the surface with soft cotton rags.

If you are thinking that a machine will give you better results, I have seen the same shine achieved by both methods.

How Many Coats of Wax?

The key to maintaining a protected surface is not how many coats of wax you put on at one time. Rather, the answer lies in how often you *compound* and wax.

Most fiberglass waxes stick to the surface, not to themselves. So, if you apply that extra coat of wax, it may fill in where the first did not, but it will not give extra protection to the surface.

How Often?

Some boat owners think just because the gelcoat is shiny it does not need to be cleaned or waxed.

Not true.

This misconception is due to the fact that most of us think that the wax makes the surface shiny when, indeed, it is the compounding that does the job. So, just because the surface of the gelcoat is shiny that does not mean that there is still wax on it, protecting it.

That is why it is very important that you have some type of compounding and waxing schedule set up for your boat so that you never give the sun the opportunity to break down the wax and, hence, the gelcoat. I recommend that compounding and waxing be done at least three times a year. If, however, you live in an area where the ultraviolet rays may not be as strong, like in some northern latitudes or you keep your boat stored in the garage, you may not need to compound and wax as often. It is best to use your better judgement.

Remember: Once the sun breaks down the wax, it will do the same to the gelcoat.

In Search of the Quick Fix

I have to admit, maintaining fiberglass gelcoat is not only time-consuming, but also physically appalling. But, for heaven's sake, do not think you are doing yourself a favor by pouring acrylic floor polish all over her. That acrylic shine will cost you more than if you would have done it right in the first place.

It looks great when you first pour it on and you will think you found the answer to a boat maintenance prayer. But, after a year, your quick fix prayer will turn into a never fix nightmare.

After the sun has had some time to work on the acrylic polish, it turns an ugly brown that does not come off easily. I would rather be the boat owner that let my gelcoat go, then the one stuck with a permanent cast of gloom.

Small Gelcoat Repairs

Preventative maintenance, protection, pride -- all these good things come about when boat owners compound and wax their boats on a regular basis. Compounding and waxing the gelcoat prevents it from becoming chalk. It protects the gelcoat from the sun's destructive rays and from other hazardous elements, such as water pollution and accidental spills. Finally, it gives boat owners a great sense of pride.

There is one other thing that should happen during the compounding and waxing phase: a serious visual inspection of your boat's gelcoat for gouges, scratches, chips and cracks. If any of these little monsters do jump out at you, do not be intimidated by them. Fix them. It is really easy!

First, the damaged area must be prepared. (Keep in mind, your job will be a lot simpler if you keep the repair area as small as possible). Clean the area. It must be free of any foreign matter so that the repair putty will take hold. If you are repairing fine scratches that cannot be rubbed out by compounding, take a sharp can opener or paint scraper and slightly gouge them out. This will provide a better filling surface. Once you are sure the wound is pretty much free of foreign particles, flush it out with water.

After the area has dried completely -- you might want to use a heater of some sort to speed up the process -- mask around it with masking tape. Then, take a #200-grit sandpaper and gently sand over the wound. Wipe with a cloth saturated with acetone. The acetone will remove any dirt and wax which would otherwise inhibit the bonding which must take place.

Now, you are ready to fill the void. Most marine hardware stores sell small tubes of gelcoat with catalyst added.

The hardest part, at this point, is going to be matching colors. If you can, go back to your boat's manufacturer and see if you can get a sample of your boat's color. If this is impossible, you can always call on a professional. What it costs you for a professional's service may not be worthwhile. It can take from fifteen minutes to three hours just to match the color.

Once you have the gelcoat putty, apply it with a putty knife. Press firmly while filling the cavity to force out any air bubbles. Make sure to over-fill the area because gelcoat has a tendency to shrink. Filling the gelcoat to the beginning of the masking tape is a good guideline to follow. Work quickly. The gelcoat putty will harden in fifteen to twenty minutes.

For gelcoat to cure properly, you must somehow seal it from the air. There are two popular methods for doing this. The first is the PVA (polyvinyl alcohol) method. It can be bought from most businesses that deal in fiberglass repair. The second method, and a much easier one for smaller jobs, is simply covering the gelcoat with wax paper or Saran Wrap. If you choose this technique, run a squeegee over the surface of the plastic wrap to get rid of any air bubbles that might be trapped inside.

After the gelcoat "kicks," i.e. hardens, remove the PVA or plastic wrap and sand with a #220-grit sandpaper. Sand carefully. It is easy to break through the new gelcoat and if you do, you will have to start over. For a high-gloss finish, continue sanding with a #400-grit wet sandpaper and then with a #600-grit sandpaper. Protect the patch by buffing it with a good carnauba-based wax.

Catalyzed gelcoat can either be applied by brush or by using an aerosol-can airbrush. For best results, use an aerosol-can airbrush. You can purchase them from any good marine hardware store and they are quite inexpensive. For the novice, especially, the difference between the two would be, perhaps, a lumpy finish produced by a brush, as apposed to a smooth finish generated by the airbrush.

In addition to the convenient tubes of gelcoat sold in marine supply stores, there are two other fillers used throughout the industry: epoxy and polyester putties.

Microballoons or a "mat," need to be added to these fillers to give them substance and strength -- resins alone are worthless. Both resins should be pigmented for color.

There are some differences between the two resins. Polyester resins cure more rapidly and are less expensive. In common practice, polyester resin has a tendency to shrink and crack in approximately a year.

Epoxy resin is more expensive, but it bonds much better to the surface than does polyester and seems to hold up a lot longer. Epoxy resin, however, is much more difficult to work with.

All in all, repairing gelcoat is an easy process. It is important, however, that you understand the difference between gelcoat repair and fiberglass repair. The above methods are only for repairs that do not cut through to the laminates beneath the gelcoat. If there are any signs of discoloration in your boat's gelcoat, there is a good possibility that the damage to the gelcoat went beneath the surface -- or, if over the weekend you happened to run into the side of your dock and you put a big hole in your fiberglass.

Do not wait until your gelcoat starts changing color. Seek a professional's advice. The damaged part of the boat's structure may have to be rebuilt. And, this is a whole new ball game.

Below-The-Waterline Blisters

Whether you keep your boat stored in or out of the water, have type A as opposed to type B hull, cruise in fresh water as opposed to saltwater, there is always the possibility that it may develop below-the-waterline blisters.

Gelcoat blistering develops when moisture becomes trapped between the gelcoat and the laminates. The moisture reacts with the watersoluable materials leftover from the curing process and creates blisters.

What causes this to happen in the first place is still speculative, but there are some theories: water pollutants, gelcoat quality, and/or poor workmanship.

If you want to maintain the integrity of your boat's hull, periodically check for blistering. If you have a bottom maintenance service, they should be doing this already. If you do not, get yourself a dive mask and a high powered underwater light and go check it out for yourself. If you find even one blister, haul the boat out and take care of the problem.

The best prevention and treatment for fiberglass blistering is to epoxy the bottom of your boat. Here is how:

Haul your boat out of the water and take it to a place where you can work on it for two days, or possibly two months. Let it dry.

Sand the hull with a #220-grit sandpaper, paying particular attention to the blistered areas. After you have opened up the blisters you must let the hull dry *completely*. The best way to tell if the hull has completely dried is to tape some plastic wrap to the hull, wait a day or so, and if the plastic wrap shows moisture, you know the hull is not completely dry.

Next, fill the cavities left from the blisters with an epoxy resin. After the epoxy has dried, sand again. The filled blisters should be sanded smooth so that there is no evidence of the holes. Coat the hull with an epoxy. Follow the recommended number of coats on the back of the manufacturer's can. After the epoxy has dried, paint over it with a good quality bottom paint.

What is important to remember about bottom blistering is, even if your boat just has one or two small blisters, it is very likely to develop more. So, the best thing you can do is to epoxy the whole hull and not just one or two spots.

Are You Expecting a Miracle?

If you have let your gelcoat go without any preventative maintenance, you can be sure it is going to cost you when you want it restored. The payment will be either physically abusing your body because you will have to get out there and drudge away, or assaulting your wallet because you will have to pay someone else to do it. There is just no way you can expect anything less.

Preventative maintenance is cheaper and does not hurt as much as paying for a miracle.

CHAPTER 7
RUNNING AND STANDING RIGGING

Sher's definition of a finely tuned rig:
"One that stands proud without fear of falling and
runs gracefully through the water like a song free of limitations."

When it comes to maintaining the rig and its counterparts, it goes without saying that a sailboat owner has greater responsibilities than those of a powerboat owner. However, for such things as lifelines, stanchions, and turnbuckles, the obligations are shared by both.

Neglect is a poor excuse for a shroud that gives way under a full sail or for lifelines that collapse under full body weight.

A Ticket Aloft

If a lack of transportation has been the only reason you have not been up to inspect the top of your mast, you have probably never heard of the "bosun's chair."

The bosun's chair has been the sailor's ticket to the top for years. It can be found in most marine hardware stores and is a **must** investment that will easily pay its own way.

When purchasing a bosun's chair, make sure it has the following features: a safety belt, made out of canvas; plenty of pockets for tools; and a wooden seat sewn into the cloth. (Modernization has really done us a favor in terms of safety, comfort, and convenience when you think back to when sailors went aloft on a piece of wood and some rope).

Remember the old saying, "There is safety in numbers." Well, if it has never applied to any aspect of your life, it does now. **Never go aloft alone.** Have at least one other person there to crank you up the mast and be there in case you need him or her. (Can you imagine spending the night fifty feet in the air clinging for your life to a mast? Me neither).

Here is some steadfast advice to follow when preparing for and going aloft:

1. You must trust that the gear pulling you up the mast will not fail. If you do not trust it completely, do not use it.

2. Do not rely solely on the shackle that connects the bosun's chair to the halyard to hold all your weight. Devise a safety line of some sort, like the one shown in the illustration on the opposite page, so you have a back-up in case of an emergency.

3. The safest halyard to go up on is an *internal halyard*, which runs inside the mast and over a sheave. I do not recommend going up on blocks which are attached to a tang outside the mast because there is no way to secure that system.

4. Do not go up on a spinnaker halyard.

5. Do not go aloft on a windy day unless you enjoy slamming up against stays, shrouds, and the mast.

6. Tie any tools to the chair with rope long enough that you can still use them. This will prevent you from dropping them on the deck or on your buddy's head below.

7. As you are being cranked aloft, keep both hands on the mast at all times.

Standing Rigging

The *standing rigging* on a sailboat is all the rigging that holds up the mast: shrouds, which hold the mast from port to starboard; stays, steady the mast from forward and aft; swaged terminal ends; turnbuckles; spreaders; chainplates; and, of course, the mast itself.

Shrouds and Stays. For the most part, dirty shrouds and stays will not fail. But, they could cause damage to other parts of the boat, like the decking and/or the sails. For example, let us take the sails that are left hanked to a dirty headstay. Dew spirals down the stay picking up the hitchhiking dirt for a traveling companion. By the time this pair hits the sails, they have turned into one big mess leaving dirty black streaks in the folds of the sails.

Also, moisture and dirt that constantly drip from shrouds and stays are the cause of those impossible to remove rust stains often found on the decking.

Thus, there are three ways to clean shrouds and stays:

1. Take a hose, a Scotch-Brite pad, and some rags aloft with you. Scrub the wiring with the pad and rinse off with fresh water. Swing fore

There is safety in numbers. Never go aloft alone.

and aft working your way down. Wipe the mast off as you go.

2. If you prefer not to take the hose up, stand on the deck and squirt the rigging enough to get most of the dirt off. Then, take a bucket of fresh water, a Scotch-Brite pad, and some rags and do as previously stated in number one.

3. If you are hauling out the boat, the shrouds and stays can easily be cleaned on land.

As you are cleaning the rigging, you should be inspecting the wiring, also. If you notice any broken wires, it is usually a sign that they need to be replaced. For the time being, however, you can put tape around them so they will not put holes in the sails or in someone's body.

Swaged Fittings. Unlike some fittings that can be attached by hand, such as the Noresman and Sta-lok types, the swaged fittings (which are most common) are secured by using a swedging machine. The machine literally marries the wire rope to the turnbuckles together forever unless, through constant neglect, they part.

These fittings should be inspected for hairline cracks and corrosion. If any of these signs occur, it means that something is going on inside the hardware that should not be and the fittings should be replaced. Also, because moisture and impurities from the stainless steel cause wear, a periodic dose of WD-40 (or the like) will help eliminate the problem.

Turnbuckles. Turnbuckles are used to apply tension to the rigging. If tightening the turnbuckles does not take up the slack, check the shrouds and stays from the mast to the chainplates for any defects.

Turnbuckles must be turned every so often or they will freeze up in one position and be useless. Lube with WD-40.

If you have turnbuckle boots or tape over the turnbuckles, do not let this stop you from inspecting the hardware. Believe it or not, the turnbuckles and their counterparts will survive if you do not cover them. They look better, too.

Chainplates. Inspect chainplates and make sure they are secured to the boat. If there is a problem, call a professional.

Masts. Whether aluminum or wood, the mast should be kept clean and inspected on a regular basis. Check the fasteners and make sure they are doing what they should. Check for cracks, something coming apart, rust and corrosion.

The sheave(s) at the top of the mast should spin freely and the surface

SAFETY SCHOOL

DON'T   DO

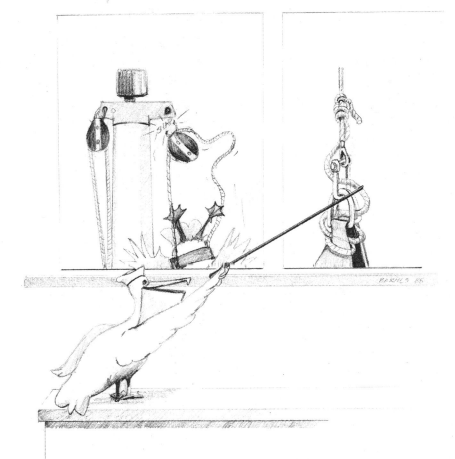

When going aloft,
DO attach a safety line from the bosun's chair to the halyard
and DO NOT go up on an external halyard.

should be smooth and free from defects that may damage the halyard. Spray occasionally with WD-40.

A wooden mast should be checked for dry rot, especially around the fittings that collect moisture.

If there are any major repairs to be done, you will stay younger if the mast is taken down and repaired on land.

Running Rigging

Running rigging is best defined as anything that moves to run the sails: halyards, sheets, winches, and blocks. All should be kept healthy enough to set and trim the sails.

Halyards. A *halyard* is the line that pulls the sails up and down. Because this line takes more strain then the others, it must be checked periodically for chafe. The best way to inspect it is to remove it from the mast by hand.

Sheets. *Sheets* adjust the sails. There are two ways to clean sheets: 1. Put sheets in a bucket of fresh water and mild detergent and stomp on them like grapes, then rinse with plenty of fresh water. 2. Put the sheets in a pillowcase, or net bag, and wash in the washing machine with a mild detergent. Let them air dry. Never put them in a dryer.

Winches. These hardworking devices deserve some tender, loving care every once in a while, at least annually.

Disassemble and soak the parts in a bucket of diesel fuel or paint thinner. After soaking, grease parts and reassemble. Watch out for the small parts and the ones that jump out at you. It is a good idea to cover scuppers so the little parts cannot abandon ship.

If you do not feel comfortable disassembling a winch, try to get hold of an owner's manual or call a professional for advice.

Blocks. Keep clean with fresh water and lubricate bearings with WD-40.

Take Your Hands Off My Lifeline

The most common reason lifelines and stanchions get loose is the eager-beaver person waiting anxiously on the dock to help you into your slip who grabs hold of them and pulls with all his or her might in a heroic effort to help you.

Every time someone pulls on this lifesaving system, it lessens the

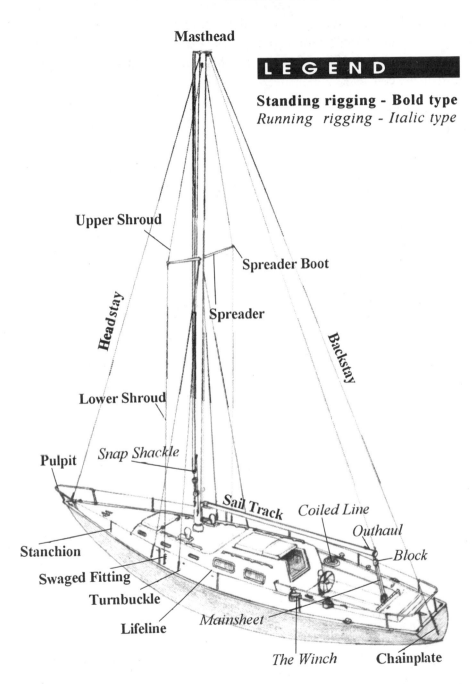

Masthead

LEGEND

Standing rigging - Bold type
Running rigging - Italic type

Upper Shroud

Spreader Boot

Headstay

Spreader

Backstay

Lower Shroud

Snap Shackle

Pulpit

Sail Track   *Coiled Line*

Outhaul

Stanchion

Block

Swaged Fitting

Turnbuckle

Lifeline

Mainsheet

The Winch   **Chainplate**

Running and Standing Rigging.

chance that a life will be saved in an emergency.

If the stanchions are loose, unbolt them from the decking, clean out the old compound, and fill in with new. Do this not only for safety reasons, but also to prevent leaks.

CHAPTER 8

SAILS AND COVERS

Sher's definition of maintaining sails and covers:
*"Keeping engines of wind from 'blowing out,' and
safekeepers made of canvas from going to the scrap pile."*

Are you using and abusing your boat's sails and covers? Do you find that the only time you pay attention to them is when you need them to power or protect your boat?

If you answered yes to these questions, this is what you have to look forward to: Cosmetic degeneration every time you hoist dirty sails and/or lay shoddy looking covers; Early breakdown of materials due to neglect; and forking out more money for items that would have lasted two to three times longer had they been properly maintained.

These inescapable facts remind me of a time I was sitting in my beach chair watching the boats go in and out of Dana Point Harbor. (One of my favorite pastimes is searching for cosmetic perfection in boats). I caught sight of a 38-foot Ericson which was in such perfect cosmetic condition that it sparkled in the sun. I was delighted to watch it motor by me, until the sails were hoisted. They were so filthy, they made the boat take on the same appearance. I could not understand the reasoning behind such a beautiful boat and the dirty sails?

Put the attitude that sails and covers do not need preventative maintenance out with next week's trash pick-up. Add them to your maintenance schedule and enjoy enhancing the looks of your boat, doubling their life and spending your money in Mexico instead of at the sailmakers or canvas shop.

Maintaining Sails

There are many types of sailcloth on the market today: Dacron (which is most widely used), Terylene, Kevlar, Mylar, and Nylon. Unfortunately,

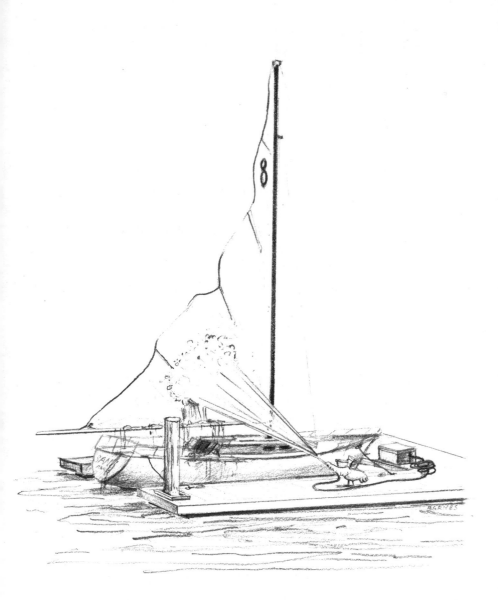

After spending time out at sea,
rinse the sails thoroughly with plenty of fresh water.
Otherwise, the salt molecules will make confetti
out of the inside of the sail cloth.

choosing one or another has nothing to do with which will hold up best. They all are engines of wind -- made out of different cloth but still battling the same destructive forces: chafing, stretching, creases and folds, moisture, dirt, mildew, salt, and overexposure to sunlight.

Sails do not require much attention to keep them safe from the above demons. The wrong kind of care, however, could be detrimental to them. As a result, educate yourself about the type of sailcloth on your boat. And, *always* handle it carefully. If you do, your sails will pay their way and bring you many hours of pure pleasure as they propel you away from reality.

Routine Rinsing. Whether racing or just cruising, the combination of sun, ocean, and excitement can sometimes deplete you of so much energy that rinsing the salt out of the sails once back into port is the last thing you want to do. If you were to look at a salt molecule under a microscope, it just might recharge your batteries.

Unseen by the naked eye are the sharp, jagged edges of a salt crystal. Magnified, one salt molecule looks like a snowflake with razor-sharp edges. When thousands of these snaggle-toothed varmints are left in the sails, they literally make confetti out of the inside of the sailcloth.

Unless you like the idea of having the inside of your sails ripped to shreds, rinse them out with plenty of fresh water after returning from a trip at sea. Maximize rinsing and let dry thoroughly before stowing.

Just in case I have not convinced you yet, if you do not rinse the salt out of your sails, one day instead of experiencing some time-out while out at sea, you may have a "blow-out" instead.

A *blow-out* is when the sails have weakened so much due to neglect (the stitching is usually the first to go) that they burst open like a worn tire on a car. And, like a flat tire, you will go nowhere with a blown-out sail, unless, of course, you carry a spare.

Washing. This section concerns sailcloth made out of Dracon. I recommend dyed sails be cleaned by a professional who specializes in them.

Sails should be taken off the boat for a thorough scrubbing at least once a season and always before stowing away for the winter.

For best results, sails should be spread flat on a clean, non-abrasive surface. Scrubbing on an abrasive surface, such as asphalt, will abrade the fibers. Unfortunately, if your boat is any bigger than a trailerboat or day-sailer, you practically need a football field made of concrete to do the job. Do not wash your sails on a lawn, doing so can cause permanent grass stains.

Scrub the sails with a soft bristle brush, using a mild non-alkaline detergent, such as Woolite or Ivory. Alkaline can make some sailcloths more sensitive to ultraviolet rays which weaken the fibers. Weak fibers attract more dirt. Because scrubbing can break down the resins in the cloth, scrub in one area only for about twenty seconds.

Stains. Instant removal of a substance which will stain the sailcloth will prevent future heartache. If, however, you do encounter a stain or two during your washing procedure, ask yourself if the stain would be better left alone rather than risking the integrity of the sailcloth.

If you want to give it a go, here is my advice on treating the most common stains found in Dacron sailcloth:

Mildew. First, remove the surface mildew using a stiff, dry bristle brush. Make a solution of bleach and fresh water (one part bleach to twenty parts fresh water). Work the solution into the stained area using your stiff bristle brush, start from the center of the stain and work outward. If you do not notice a reaction, try soaking the area in the solution for two to three hours. Rinse with plenty of fresh water.

Grease and Oil. Rub over the stain with a stain remover that contains *trichlorocthane*, such as Renuzit or Energine. Rinse thoroughly with fresh water.

Rust Stains. Soak the stained section of the sail in a solution of oxalic acid and fresh water (one part oxalic acid to ten parts fresh water). Rinse with fresh water.

Hosing Off and Drying. After washing, sails should be hung as if from a clothesline so they can be rinsed thoroughly and dried naturally. Be sure to hang the sails by the luff so that their weight is supported rather than stretched. (See the illustration on page 93).

When rinsing, use five times more water than you feel is necessary. You want to be sure all traces of detergent are out of the sails. To help combat against mildew, let the sails dry completely before stowing them.

While the sails are hanging around is a great time to get a pen and paper and inspect them for the following: chafing, unusual wear, loose stitching, and/or any tears or holes. If any repairs are needed, take the sails to your local sail loft to have them repaired. This way they will be ready to go the next time you are.

Stowing. There are four things to remember when stowing your sails:

*Wash sails on a clean, non-abrasive surface
and hang to dry properly.*

*Your sails will be around a lot longer if they are flaked
properly before stowing.*

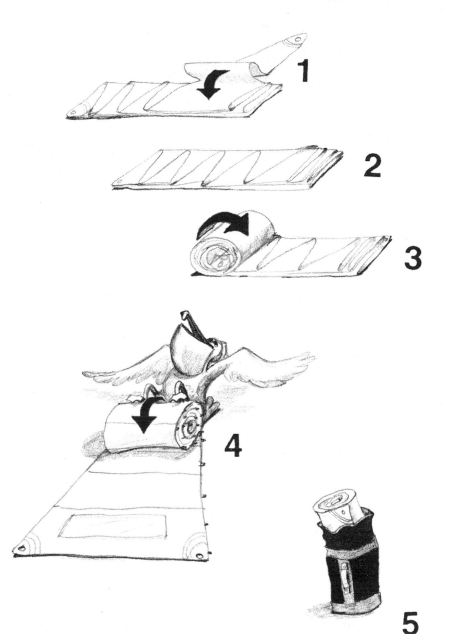

Fold sails correctly before putting them into their sail bag.
Cramming them only causes creases
which reduces their effectiveness.

1. Be sure they are clean and dry.
2. Be sure they are properly "flaked." (See the illustration on page 94).
3. Be sure they are kept covered -- always.
4. Do not ignore the need for minor repairs. Neglected minor repairs always turn into haunting major ones.

Never cram sails into their sail bags. Doing so will cause the sails to develop creases and folds which reduce their effectiveness. And, **no**, you cannot iron them out like a piece of clothing! (For illustration on how to properly fold your sails, see page 95).

Dirty Rigging . . . Clean Sails?

It may be a good idea to incorporate cleaning the rigging with washing your sails. It could be quite disheartening to watch your snowy white sails lay up against dirty black shrouds. (See Chapter 7, *Running and Standing Rigging*).

Protecting Canvas Safekeepers

I knew of a boat owner who thought the easiest way to wash his canvas covers was to take them to the neighborhood Laundromat.

After such a brutal experience, the covers had shrunk so much that the only boat they might fit was Barbie and Ken's.

It is OK if you want to put small covers (winch, compass, binnacle) into the washer, delicate cycle. But do not dry them in the dryer! Hang them out to air dry.

Wash the larger covers as you would your sails. Spread them out on a clean, non-abrasive surface and scrub with a brush and mild detergent. Hang, rinse thoroughly with fresh water, and let air dry.

Once a month, vacuum covers to get rid of dust that would otherwise accumulate and turn to muck.

If the covers are brand new, or in good condition, treat them with a fabric protector such as Scotchgard. The fabric still is allowed to breath while whatever lands on them will adhere to the resistor rather then the fabric. By the way, did you know that acids in bird guano bleach canvas.

Having your covers treated will make maintaining them 100% easier. They will last longer and they will not have bleached out imprints of bird droppings on them.

Pick Up and Deliver

Were you aware that in some areas of the United States of America, there are companies that will pick up dirty sails and covers, wash and dry them, and then return them to the customer in a neat clean package? I was not either until recently.

In researching information for this chapter, I learned of a company in Newport Beach, California, called Aqua Marine, which was more than generous in providing me with additional information on how to care for sails and covers.

If you are unable to maintain your own sails and covers, I highly recommend using a company such as Aqua Marine. I know that time and space to lay out the sails are major factors that limit boat owners in doing the maintenance themselves. But, these are not problems for these professionals who are in the business of preserving the life of your sails and covers.

*Do not let your first introduction to your bilge
be a wet one.*

CHAPTER 9

OH YEAH. . .
THE BILGE

Sher's definition of a clean religiously inspected bilge:
"Peace of mind knowing that you will not be sharing below deck with
horrendous odors or an unexpected high tide."

When it comes to maintenance, if the bilge on a boat is overlooked, it is usually for one or all of these reasons: 1. It has a stink-hole reputation and nobody wants to go near it. 2. It is camouflaged by floorboards and nobody knows it exists. 3. There is no access to it.

An ignored bilge, however, has ways of getting its owner's attention. For example, one bilge introduced itself to its owner by emitting odors so bad the owner's guests were green with seasickness. All the bilge meant to tell the owner was that the head pipe had sprung a leak.

Another bilge made its existence known to the boat owner because a shower-through hull clamp had been allowed to rust away. One morning the boat owner came down to the dock to find his boat under five feet of water.

A bilge should not have to put its owner through such distressing experiences as these to get some attention. Keep in mind that a bilge is only a "stink-hole" because the owner keeps it that way. If the reason is because there is no access to it, make one.

There is no excuse for unpleasant smells or boats that list, especially because most bilges can be self-cleaning. It just does not take much effort to hold a regular flashlight and open your eyes to see to it that it is well-maintained.

Cleaning the Bilge

The two most important reasons to keep the bilge clean are to prevent bacteria growth and bad odors.

Marine hardware stores sell a bilge cleaner that works well, but it can be costly. I have found that using liquid Tide is much cheaper and it does a great job. It contains no phosphorus, is biodegradable, cuts into grease and dirt, and to top it off, it has a wonderful, clean smell.

Some boats take in more water then others. If the boat you are concerned with usually has water in its bilge, add the liquid Tide and let the rock and roll of the boat do the cleaning for you. (Be sure you know that the water the boat is taking in is not coming from a leaking through-hull fitting or pipe. If it is, replace the defective part).

Do not allow water to remain in the bilge for prolonged periods. It can cause rust, mildew, and peel paint. Besides, IT STINKS!

Limber Holes. These are ducts located in the bilge which allow water to pass through them and flow to the lowest point of the bilge where it will be pumped out either manually or automatically.

It is essential that these ducts be kept clear of residue which may block the passage of water. Otherwise, you will have a fine mess to clean up.

Engine Oil Drips. Hopefully, before someone installed the engine(s) in your boat, they were thoughtful enough to put down an oil drip pan first. If not, any oil dripping from the engine goes into the bilge instead of the pan.

Whether you are changing the oil, cleaning oil from a drip pan, or chasing oil leaks down the bilge, there are two items that work the best in absorbing the oil: feminine napkins and disposable diapers. Use whichever one you are least embarrassed to purchase and the one easiest to explain to curious neighbors!

Inspecting the Bilge

A bilge and its surroundings should be inspected once a month with a flashlight. Here is a list of things to look for in an honest visual inspection:

1. Unusual amounts of water should be traced to the source of leakage.

2. Check the float arm on an electric bilge pump. Lift it up and make sure it is functional.

3. Check through-hull openings and fittings. Make sure fittings are

secure and in good shape. I have heard horror stories of boats sinking just because a through-hull fitting came loose.

4. Seacocks should be opened and closed to insure that they are working properly.

5. Look for corrosion everywhere and check for any unusual growth.

6. Check pipes, hoses, and clamps.

7. If the boat is wooden, check for wood rot.

8. Check limber holes.

Steam Cleaning

Normally, most grease and dirt can be removed with some detergent and elbow grease. If, however, you are not willing to succumb to that method of cleaning, steam is an alternative.

Steam cleaning is a harsh method that can cause paint to peel, especially on a wooden boat

I recommend you do not try it yourself. Instead, call a professional, ask them questions, and call their references.

Do Not Dump In The Bay!

Discharging waste into the bay is something children might do just because they did not know any better. Threats are things we use to try to get the children not to pollute the bay any further. We use tactics like putting dye in the boat's holding tank so when there is a discharge, we know from which boat it came. Or, we mark the boats with no holding tanks so we can monitor them.

Using pumpouts to dispose of waste is something mature caring adults do. Adults who do not feel that there are enough pumpouts to service the whole harbor, should go to city council meetings and voice their opinions.

An adult boat owner loves the ocean and realizes polluting it is an act of contempt or carelessness. Even a child knows contempt or apathy can be harmful. We all need to act as adults.

It is too important not to care.

Save steps by cleaning one room at a time.

CHAPTER 10

INTERIORS

Sher's definition of a boat's interior:
"A buoyant feeling of being home."

Unlike the exterior of a boat that is always fighting the harmful elements of a marine environment, an interior's only battle is with its owner.

A good example of this is the time we were asked to go to Dana Point Harbor and clean a 42-foot Westsail. The outside of the boat was not too bad, but when we opened the hatch and looked inside, our first reactions were to close the hatch and sneak out of the harbor. In hindsight, we should have.

Instead, we spent hours below doing what we do best -- cleaning. We chiseled at the ring around the inside of the toilet bowl, went through two cans of Endust, and magically turned musty odors into pleasant smells.

We were proud of our wizardry. The boat owner, on the other hand, was appalled. His interior was *too* clean!

This unhappy event taught us early on that one person's eyesore may be another's delight. If you are a boat owner thinking about having someone maintain your interior, tell him or her before they start what you are comfortable with. If, however, you are going to be doing the cleaning -- ask before you start what the owner prefers. This should apply to the exterior as well. Being up front at the beginning is better then being in an uncomfortable situation at the end.

Stand By for Efficiency Below

Make a list of cleaning supplies you will need for a particular interior, get yourself a caddy, and put them inside it.

Take your caddy brimming with cleaning supplies by the handle and go into one room. Clean the entire room. Go to the next room and do the same. Start aft and work your way forward or vice versa.

Cleaning one room at a time is not only efficient, but you will have more energy when you are through to go topside and pick a fight with a sea gull.

Windows and Mirrors

Same as the exterior. Vinegar and fresh water for the glass. Plastic polish for the plastic ports. Some mirrors also are made of plastic.

Vacuum and lubricate runners, if needed. Do not forget about the glass clocks, barometers, and control panels. Little details make a big difference.

Curtains

Vacuum the curtains on a regular basis. Most curtains can be dry cleaned or machine washed on a delicate cycle.

If during a rain storm, water spots beat you to the curtains before you had time to close the windows, here is what you should do: Place a damp rag under the spot and rub the area with another damp rag from the other side working from the center of the stain outward.

Upholstery

Vacuum all the upholstery periodically. Take the cushions off and vacuum underneath for crumbs and cobwebs. Wipe up spills with detergent and fresh water before they dry.

Carpet

The more a carpet is walked on, the more it should be vacuumed. If not, the dirt and sand will grind into the fibers and wear it down.

Keep some commercial spot remover handy. Most brands work well. Wipe up the little spots before they turn into one gigantic one. If, however, the carpet is already bad, hire a professional to clean it.

If you are the type that likes to go to supermarket and rent a carpet cleaning machine, be sure to get all the water up from the carpet and let it dry thoroughly before people start walking on it. Any water left in the fibers of the carpet will attract dirt like a magnet attracts metal. Furthermore, it has been my experience that once carpets are cleaned with detergent and water, they get dirtier quicker. So, you may want to consult a professional about your options.

Combat interior mildew by circulating air with a fan
and leaving a light on.

Do Yourself a Favor: Scotchgard

If you are tired of seeing little Joey's Coke soak into the furniture and carpet, Scotchgard them. Scotchgard is a fabric protector and the greatest invention next to the boat. It is an interior's guardian angel because it makes little beads out of foreign liquid matter which allows you to wipe it up before it dries into the fabric.

Read the manufacturer's directions and warnings on the back of the can.

The Galley

This is one area where it is better to throw away a mess rather than have to clean it up. Take some aluminum foil and line the shelves in the refrigerator, the top of the stove, and the bottom of the oven.

The refrigerator. Clean with white vinegar. Doing so will cut grease, kill mildew, and remove odors. There is no need to rinse.

If the refrigerator is not going to be used for a while, turn it off and leave the door open for ventilation. Secure the open door so it does not close or cause damage to surrounding surfaces.

Stainless Steel Sinks. These sinks should be kept like the outside of the boat: clean, dry, and waxed.

Rust can usually be found in this area, but it is not the sink's fault. The rust is caused by leaving metal utensils in the sink. To remove the rust, use a mild abrasive or a rust remover. Flush with detergent and fresh water and dry. After the sinks are good and dry, you can either wax them or spray them with Endust, this will help to prevent the return of rust.

Counter Tops. Wipe down counter tops with detergent and fresh water, then dry. Going over these surfaces with Endust gives a shiny clean effect to young and old counter tops alike.

The Head

Clean the head, basin, and shower with liquid Lysol. Waxing the toilet bowl and shower after they are dry will keep them clean and make maintenance easier. Put a rubber mat in the shower after waxing.

Pour a cap-full of liquid Lysol into the toilet bowl to help prevent odors. Spray the entire area with Lysol to help prevent mildew.

Mates, leave your dirt at the door.

Vinyl Overheads

Imagine being sentenced to a life as a vinyl overhead: You cannot move. From below you, comes clouds of cigarette smoke, the cooking odors of a bad cook, and every once and a while, you are hit by a flying champagne cork. As a result, you begin to turn yellow because life as a vinyl overhead just is not worth living.

On a more serious note, nothing can keep a vinyl overhead from its natural deterioration process, but something can slow it down: a good vinyl cleaner/restorer.

Varnished Trim

Trim that has been finished is virtually maintenance free and should last years if the wood beneath it does not get wet. Wipe occasionally with Endust or any good furniture polish.

Unfinished Trim

Liquid Gold works great on bare wood. It cleans and oils at the same time. We also found that Liquid Gold hides a lot of flaws that might be in the wood. If, on the other hand, you want something that is going to harden, use linseed oil. Do not use dressings meant for exterior use. They contain strong volatiles that may harm you.

Lurking Mildew

Are the eyes of mildew upon you? If they are, it is because there are some damp, dark, musty places to hide in such as drawers and bulkheads.

Eliminate the mildew with X-14 mildew remover. Test an inconspicuous area first. Then get yourself a small fan and a light bulb for the interior. The fan will keep the air circulating, but be sure to secure it so it cannot fall. The light bulb is for dry heat. If your boat is docked, it is a good idea to have the electrical dock supply checked for leakage by a professional. This will help to eliminate electrolytic corrosion. (For more details, see Chapter 11, *A Tip Top Bottom*).

When the boat is not in use, open compartments and take out any wet articles, such as bathing suits and life jackets. To keep clothes and linens fresh on the boat, place fabric softener sheets in the drawers and closets.

Odors Down Under

To freshen the air, set a bowl(s) of vinegar out while the boat is taking a break from entertaining. Be sure that the bowls are secure and the vinegar cannot spill from them.

Leave the Dirt at the Door

Place a vinyl/rubber backed mat in front of the entrance to the interior with a sign above if that reads: "Wipe 'em off or take 'em off."

Cannot Blame it on the Sun

Protect the interior from the sun's ultraviolet rays by installing window covers, or pull the curtains shut when the boat is just sitting.

The little energy spent protecting your boat's interior will save you from having to replace a teak veneer dash and/or faded carpet which could cost you untold dollars.

If you are unable to find a fish to spy on your diver, ask your bottom service to provide you with a video inspection of your boat's bottom.

CHAPTER 11

A TIP TOP BOTTOM

Sher's definition of below the waterline maintenance:
"Helping wood, fiberglass, and metal hardware survive life
submerged in a giant battery."

For the most part, hull maintenance is given low priority because the hull floats silently out of sight and out of mind. Boat owners are unaware of the damage that is being caused to their hulls, especially in the warm summer months. The ruination happens in slow, progressive degree like an architect planning a marina.

First, slime sets its sights on a clean hull and establishes a foundation for grass and seaweed. After the weeds have grown thick like a carpet, the barnacles take root and embed themselves stubbornly into the structure of the hull. Now what we have is a little underwater marina screaming out to such things as slugs, mussels, and water roaches -- beckoning them to come and moor.

Given such a scenario, the two most important reasons to keep the bottom of your boat properly cleaned and thoroughly inspected are for safety and performance.

For safety's sake, the middle of the ocean is not the place you want to be when you learn that your boat has a cracked prop. Imagine your wife, or someone dear to you, having to do the last three miles to Catalina dog-paddling.

In terms of performance, if there is growth clinging to the hull of your boat, it can cut down your fuel consumption 5-30%, depending upon the amount of growth.

The bottom line is: Do not let down the bottom of your boat because it is liable to do the same to you out in the middle of nowhere.

A Fish's Eye View

The greatest disadvantage a boat owner has with an underwater service is the inability to check his or her work.

Would it not be great if we could jump into the bay, turn into fishes just as we hit the water (like Mr. Limpet) and watch our divers do their thing?

Let us pretend for just a moment that we can do just that -- be fishes incognito.

If the diver in front of us servicing the sailboat is a true professional, he should be able to pass the checklist below:

☐ He is equipped with the following supplies: a stainless steel sponge, a scraper with a stiff blade, a piece of thick carpet, a Scotch-Brite pad, a screw driver, and (of course) a source of air.

☐ If he is wearing tanks, he knows to always face the boat so he will not damage the hull with them.

☐ He uses his wet suit for buoyancy and adjusts his weights so he is pressed up against the hull about forehead level. He does not fight to stay down nor sink to the bottom.

☐ The professional always cleans by sight, not by touch.

☐ He cleans by using vertical/horizontal motions as opposed to circular.

☐ He uses the least abrasive material he can to clean the hull.

☐ As he cleans the hull, he clears the through-hulls, the knot meter, the raw water intake valve, and the depth sounder of any growth that might be blocking their openings.

☐ He checks the hull for blisters and the metal hardware for cracks and electrolysis.

☐ He studies the zinc carefully for corrosion and will replace it if necessary.

☐ He polishes the prop and shaft with his stainless steel sponge.

☐ After he is done, he swims around the hull again to double check his work.

Of course, our being fish watching a diver clean the bottom of our boat is all make-believe. But, the list is a reality and had better be for all professional divers. (Maybe Mr. Limpet would like a spying job working for the federation of boat owners?)

How Often

In conditions like we have here in Southern California, every seventy-two hours something microscopic drops anchor on the hull of a boat and starts to grow there. In the winter, the growth rate is less.

With the exception of wood boats, professionals suggest that hulls be serviced every month during the summer and every other month during the winter, provided that the boats are kept in the water. Wooden boats, however, should be serviced less because of their softer paint, every other month during the summer and every three to four months during the winter.

If you are uncertain about the schedule your boat should be on, call different diving companies and ask questions, ask questions, ask questions!

"The Dry Diver"

This is a device which allows the boat owner to clean the bottom without getting wet. The instrument is comprised of a series of scrub brushes with foam floats attached to them. The device conforms to the side of the hull and when pushed down into the water, it tries to force its way back up causing a scrubbing-like action. It can be purchased in most marine hardware stores for about $80.00.

I suppose the invention is a good idea if you only want half the job done. I believe it is far better to have a wet professional diver then it is to have an amateur dry one.

These are my reasons:

1. You stay dry but you cannot see what you are cleaning.

2. The "Dry Diver" does only a marginal job.

3. The "Dry Diver" does not give you a personal inspection of the hull and its hardware.

4. The "Dry Diver" does not know how to change the prop.

5. The "Dry Diver" does not know what electrolysis looks like, nor could it tell you if it did.

"Bagging" Your Boat

This is not the system for the boat owner who just wants to get into his or her boat, start the engine, and get the heck away from reality.

The procedure is such that the boat actually sits in a bag filled with chemicals which prevent bottom growth and a quick escape. Hence, every time you wanted to use your boat, you would have to untie the bag, drive

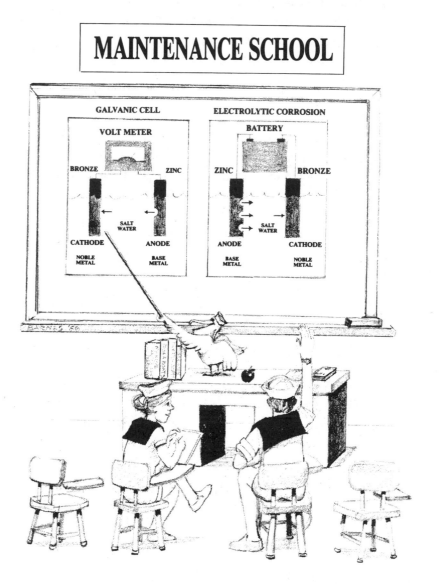

*A brief education in electrolysis
(the corrosion process of metals)
will help you provide longer lives to metal hardware.*

the boat out, and tie the bag up again. I understand it works well but is not worth the inconvenience it causes.

There has also been some concern expressed by the Environmental Protection Agency that the bags may be polluting the water, either by the chemicals or by the bag sinking to the bottom of the bay and being left to deteriorate into unhealthy tidbits for marine life. Studies are still being done.

A Layperson's Look at Electrolysis

In my attempt to understand a phenomenon such as electrolysis (the corrosion process of metals), I had to keep reminding myself that the problem stemmed from two totally different sources:

A giant God-given battery -- the ocean -- which will never die, unless man kills it; and a man-made electrical source which will never survive, unless man keeps it alive.

Galvanic Corrosion. This corrosion is caused by the giant God-given battery, the ocean.

When two dissimilar metals are placed into this sea of energy, an electrical current is generated between them and the birth of corrosion is the result. In this process, the weaker of the metals, such as zinc, which is also known as the *base* metal, will dissolve so that the stronger metal, such as bronze the *noble* metal, can survive and do the job it is intended to do, like propel the boat through the water.

Electrolytic Corrosion. This corrosion is caused by a man-made electrical current which has gone awry or "stray."

These wandering destructive currents usually emerge from an external source such as the boat's battery or from a shore power supply box which has a poorly installed electrical circuit.

Larger powerboats and any boat which happens to be docked next to them suffer greatly from this type of corrosion due to their need to run more electricity than most sailboats.

Electrolytic corrosion is stronger than galvanic corrosion in that it will drive a more nobel metal to corrode which normally would not under galvanic conditions.

The most critical point to be made about electrolytic corrosion is that one must be aware that the stray current can either be dribbling like a stream or gushing like a waterfall.

The Recipe for Corrosion

(Serves Millions)

An Electrolyte
(The ocean because it can conduct electricity)

A Cathode
(A noble metal such as bronze)

An Anode
(A base metal such as zinc)

This recipe works the best when the electrolyte is warm and salty. Fresh water will not do. Because we are using the ocean as our electrolyte, it will move naturally and produce a great electrical current. Add the cathode and anode, bronze and zinc are the favorites, to the electrolyte and bond them together. Corrosion will follow. Variations can be made as to which cathode and anode to use but it is imperative that the correct ones be chosen. (See *Galvanic Survivors and Protectors* on the opposite page).

Incidentally, this recipe is disliked all over the world.

Cathodic Protection

If we did not have the anodes to protect the cathodes from corrosion, we would be like the little Dutch boy with his finger in the side of the dike trying to keep it from bursting.

There are a number of methods used today, but the most popular is the use of a *sacrificial anode*. A sacrificial anode is a base metal purposely connected to a noble metal (or the cathode) to protect it. The sacrificial anode will gradually corrode while protecting the cathode.

Galvanic Survivors and Protectors

1. High Chromium
   Stainless Steel
2. Nickel-Copper Alloy
3. Copper-Nickel Alloy
4. Bronze (popular noble metal)
5. Copper
6. Brass
7. Tin
8. Lead
9. Lead-Tin Solder

10. Low-Chromium
    Stainless Steel
11. Cast Iron
12. Wrought Iron
13. Mild Steel
14. Cadmium
15. Aluminum
16. Zinc (most commonly used
    base metal)
17. Magnesium

This is a list of metals most commonly used in the boat-building industry. They are listed in order of their ability to resist corrosion in saltwater. Starting from the top with the noble metals which survive electrolysis when they are protected by the base metals below. For example, if zinc and bronze are joined together (bonded), the zinc will corrode to save the bronze.

The most common sacrificial anode used is zinc because it corrodes most rapidly in saltwater. This is the way the process works: The sacrificial anode is electrically joined to a noble metal, such as bronze. For example, placing a zinc rudder disc to a bronze rudder. The zinc will corrode while the bronze rudder is protected. When the zinc is consumed, it must be replaced.

The longevity of the zinc depends on the area in which the boat is docked.

Oddly enough, zinc is the least expensive of all the metals but can save you the most money. A prop can cost hundreds of dollars to replace, whereas installing zinc to preserve it only costs pennies.

Preventing Electrolytic Corrosion

Preventing this type of corrosion is a matter of good electrical wiring. For your sake and your neighbors' have a professional technician come out and survey your boat and dock for possible electrical leakage. They have a sensitive meter which will tell them immediately if you have an electrical leak.

Discouraging Galvanic Corrosion

Because galvanic corrosion is a natural event and not man-made, it will be around for many years. If we want to continue to enjoy boating, we must continue to control this process by:

1. Attempting to make all parts of an item from the same metal.

2. If metals need to be mixed, which is usually the case, make the more important items, like the fastenings, the more noble metals.

3. Electrically insulate the different metals.

4. The anode must be thick enough to allow for corrosion.

5. Make yourself aware of any stray currents from your boat and your neighbor's boat.

6. Do not paint the anode. It will not corrode if you do.

7. Do not paint metal hardware. It cannot be inspected properly if you do.

Freshwater Scum

Freshwater is less conductive than saltwater and causes little or no corrosion.

But, freshwater can cause hard water build-up if the boat is left in the water for a prolonged period or is not hosed off after being taken out of the water.

If compounding does not remove the build-up, try Lime Away or muriatic acid. Test an inconspicuous area first and use plenty of freshwater to rinse the boat. Re-wax after the hard water build-up has been removed.

The Boat Owner versus The Professional Diver

Whether you clean the bottom of the boat yourself or hire a professional, it is best to know what is going on, on the hull of your boat. The bottom of your boat is the last thing you want to be uneducated about.

If you are thinking of hiring a diver, here are some guidelines to follow before you trust him or her with the bottom of your boat:

1. How long has he or she been diving/cleaning?

2. Ask for references and follow through with phone calls to them.

3. Ask reputable boat yards for advice and assistance. After all, they see bottoms all the time.

4. Ask the diver to define electrolysis and its prevention.

5. Ask the diver to explain his or her cleaning procedure and tools used.

CHAPTER *12*

DOCK RAT BITS

Sher's definition of dock rat bits:
"Little pieces of advice taken from
the mouths of waterfront authorities.''

The following quotes have been graciously given to me by many different sorts of "dock rats:" boat maintenance workers, boat owners, divers, sail cleaners, and boat brokers, to name a few. I found these people scurrying about such harbors as Newport Beach, Long Beach, San Pedro, Friday Harbor and Nanaimo, British Columbia, Canada.

These words of wisdom were given so that you might learn from their experience instead of learning the hard way.

"In today's world of yachts, the appearance of canvas work has become increasingly important. The function of boat covers is many times placed in a secondary role. Proper canvas work, where function is not forgotten, can save a boat owner untold dollars in maintenance costs and add dramatically to the life of varnish work and other sun-sensitive areas of your boat. Cover up! Good canvas work is worth every dollar you pay for it."

-Don Thomas, V.P., General Manager
Blinn & Young, Inc., Newport Beach, California

"If you are curious about the condition of the bottom of your boat and do not want or need to haul it out, ask your diving service to provide you with a video inspection."

-Jose A. Acevedo
Long Beach, California

"As a boat maintenance worker, the best advice I can give a boat owner is to wash his or her boat weekly and rinse it down after each use to remove the saltwater. Leaving the salt on the boat will eventually cause cosmetic damage. To make the job easier, use such tools as: a squeegee, a nozzle for the hose, an extension pole with a soft scrub brush, and an absorber (synthetic chamois). Remember that all the products you use on your boat roam throughout the bay and eventually flow into our ocean. Try to use biodegradable products whenever possible so that you don't choke the fish and birds."

-Bonnie Haines
Newport Beach, California

"It has been my experience that maintenance performed on a regular basis, at least once a week, is crucial if the yacht owner is to avoid costly service expenses due to normal wear and tear induced by the elements and normal recreational use."

-Robert Dair
Newport Beach, California

"Maintenance should be considered an additional monthly expense before the purchase of a boat. It is common that the boat owner realizes the extra expense after the fact and finds that it does not fit into his or her budget which causes the new investment to depreciate rapidly."

-Shari Woodbridge
Laguna Beach, California

"If you fish out of your boat, continuously rinse it off while you are out at sea with a bucket of water from the ocean and be sure to hose it down good when you return to the dock. If you don't, it makes for a long, hard cleaning job for you or your cleaning crew."

-Lynn Hunter
Long Beach, California

"Let's stay ahead of the game instead of worrying about it until it breaks."

-KC Underwater Yacht Service
Newport Beach, California

"A boat is like a wife . . . it seemed like a good idea at the time."
-Brian Eckford
Huntington Beach, California

"All through-hull valves should be exercised\periodically to keep them working smoothly. Proper maintenance will prolong battery life. Keep batteries clean and topped up with water and DO NOT overcharge them. A good preventive maintenance program will keep your boat in the shape you want it and in the long run, will cost less than remedial maintenance."
-David Tharp
San Diego, California

"In regard to the Evinrude 9.9 1975-1976 engines, only use Evinrude oil which helps reduce replacement coils."
-Richard L. Henderson
Nanaimo, British Columbia, Canada

"If you are not going to be using your boat, but will be leaving it in the water, wrap a garbage bag around the leg of the engine to protect it from growth buildup. Put a reminder of some sort next to the ignition switch so you remember to remove it before turning the engine on."
-Pat Johnstone, Tackle & Marina
Nanaimo, British Columbia, Canada

"Don't leave fishing bait in a refrigerator that has been turned off. The smell it leaves is horrendous and virtually impossible to get rid of."
-Bonnie Johnstone
Nanaimo, British Columbia, Canada

"Don't hire cheap, unsupervised amateurs to do a professional's job. You will only end up paying twice for the same job. Once for the unprofessional and then again for the professional to come out and fix what the amateur should have done correctly in the first place."
-Southern Cross Yacht Systems
Newport Beach, California

"If you have varnish on your boat, keep it on a ninety to one hundred day maintenance schedule. If you keep it maintained, it won't go bad. The big expense is fixing the neglected varnish, not maintaining the good stuff."

-Bruce Cunard
Newport Beach, California

"Boat owners should realize the large investment wrapped up in sails and covers. Having them regularly cleaned should be considered preventive maintenance which will save them from costly unforseen damages."

-Aqua Marine
Newport Beach, California

"Preventive maintenance is the magic number one but the bottom line is -- have lots of money."

-Chuck Reed
Newport Beach, California

"Educate yourself so you can relate to the people working on every aspect of your boat. Understanding what they are talking about eliminates you from being buffaloed by them."

-Odessey Diving
Newport Beach, California

"Since the early seventies, the use of vinyl decal accent stripes has become the most common means of adding color striping to boats. While this method is not as permanent as colors molded in the gelcoat, it does have its advantages should the striping be scratched. Scratching across multiple colors of gelcoat is very difficult to repair, requires a professional to do, and generally is hard to match the existing gel, as it is probably faded. To repair decal striping, you can do the job yourself and get good results following these steps:

1. Using a sharp razor, remove only a small section around the damaged area cutting on a diagonal line across the tape.

2. Peel damaged tape away. If it does not come off easily, use a heat gun or blow dyer to soften the tape. Do not overheat. It the tape leaves a glue residue, clean it with acetone or lacquer thinner.

3. Apply new tape making sure to cut on the same diagonal lines as the old tape was cut. Overlap the tape lightly over the old to allow for shrinkage.

4. The repair is complete. Remember, up close the repair may be noticeable to you, but from a short distance back, the repair will look considerably better than the old scratched material.''

-Eric Rankin
Newport Beach, California

''I find great pleasure in boarding a clean, beautifully maintained boat and pride in showing her off. The only feeling I get from a neglected boat is embarrassment.''

-Smitty
Friday Harbor, Washington

''Anodizing is quite inexpensive and lasts longer than paint. And for the boat owner who is tired of replacing parts and looking at corroded aluminum, anodizing is the way to go. Also, a boat owner can have his or her aluminum dyed red, blue, gold, or black.''

-John Bailey
Dunham Metal Finishing, Orange, California

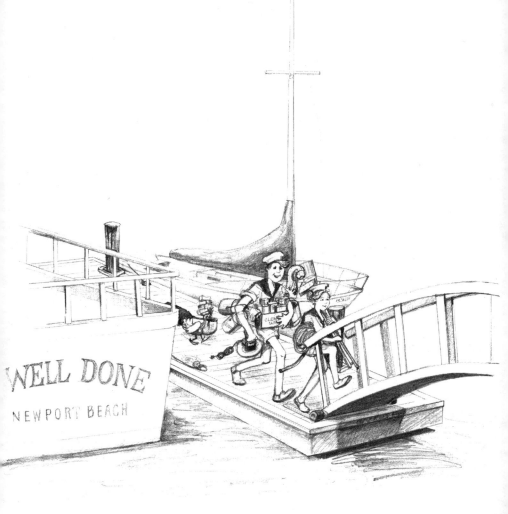

Good job mates.

NOTES:

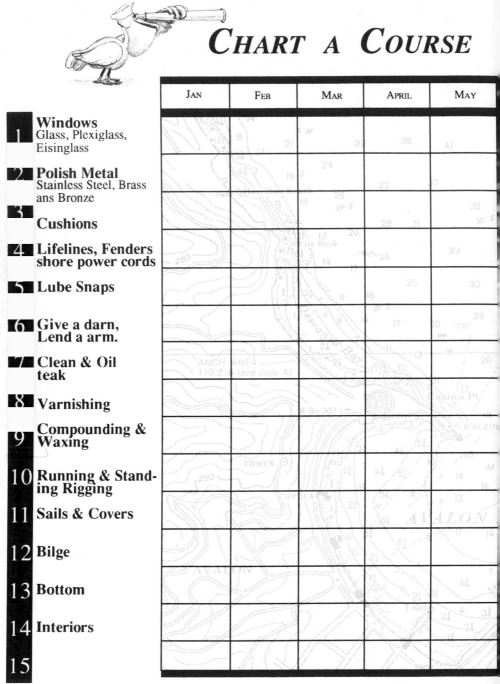

CHART A COURSE

	JAN	FEB	MAR	APRIL	MAY
1 Windows — Glass, Plexiglass, Eisinglass					
2 Polish Metal — Stainless Steel, Brass ans Bronze					
3 Cushions					
4 Lifelines, Fenders shore power cords					
5 Lube Snaps					
6 Give a darn, Lend a arm.					
7 Clean & Oil teak					
8 Varnishing					
9 Compounding & Waxing					
10 Running & Standing Rigging					
11 Sails & Covers					
12 Bilge					
13 Bottom					
14 Interiors					
15					

TO A BEAUTIFUL BOAT

JUNE	JULY	AUGUST	SEPT	OCT	NOV	DEC

INDEX